Metaethical Business Propositions

Series in 'Theories and Practices in Metaethics'

—A Book of Metaethics [Andrew Minase, Writers Club Press, 2001, ISBN: 0-595-14467-5]

—Metaethical Business Propositions [Andrew Minase, Writers Club Press, 2003, ISBN: 0-595-26469-7]

—Matters to Metaethics [Andrew Minase, Not Published Yet]

Metaethical Business Propositions

Art of Sound Business Affairs
FROM Personal Dilemma TO Management TO Society & Environment

Andrew Minase
Author of *A Book of Metaethics*

Writers Club Press
New York Lincoln Shanghai

Metaethical Business Propositions
Art of Sound Business Affairs

Writers Club Press
an imprint of iUniverse, Inc.

For information address:
iUniverse
2021 Pine Lake Road, Suite 100
Lincoln, NE 68512
www.iuniverse.com

Part of the texts in this book has oroginally appeared in an online publication, cause [ISSN: 1524-6906], since June, 1996.
The original texts are available at the wbsite: http://www.metaethics.org.

Cover Design by Andrew Minase

ISBN: 0-595-26469-7

Printed in the United States of America

Contents

Table of Contents with Summary

I. Philosophy of Metaethical Leadership

Introduction to Philosophy of Metaethical Leadership
Causes of Managerial Ethics
Ethics in business is a matter of choice by sufficient and necessary reasoning, and the method of incorporating its own business ethics is essentially a matter of *if*, not *when*. In metaethics, managerial ethics is measurable by the degree of causes that result in aspiration and commitment. The essence of management responsibility represents the power of knowledge that sustains the company's causes to serve its community. The causes of managerial ethics are measurable by the authenticity of such decision-making knowledge, which makes the company's choice sufficient and necessary, and its moral justification valid and sound.

1. Difference between Authority and Responsibility
In the Context of Managing a Business Structure
Responsibility lies where authority stands. The responsibility of a subject that is to obtain such authority is a responsibility of representation, or of representing true knowledge. Comparing philosophical authority and legal or any other kinds of authority, there is a striking difference in the certitude for an individual with authority to relate to the true knowledge at its representation. Confusion of whatever authority one may be given with one's absolute, moral authority may result in making of a poor controller of causes within an organization.

2. On Definition of Business Ethics
Understanding of Authority and Responsibility
Concepts of ethics necessitate a set of standards by which a group or community decides to regulate its behavior, distinguishably as what is legitimate and acceptable in pursuit of one's aims. In reality, the search for a grand, unifying principle of management morality often leads to frustration and doubt. The moral dilemmas that many managers face are, in essence, clashes among different spheres of responsibility. Here, the clear understanding and differentiation of authority and responsibility that each moral agent holds in every situation, must be the starting point of defining business ethics.

3. On Leadership and Ethics
Can Managers Be Good Leaders with or without Ethics?
Use of ethics in business is subjective, and also subject to change by the contexts. A decision is either morally justifiable, or it is acceptable when morally irrelevant. The former is good for leaders and managers *with* ethics; the latter is good *without* ethics. One must define the legitimacy of one's moral concerns, *i.e.*, at what point one must raise his or her own moral concerns that would be everybody else's business.

4. Moral Use of Authority and Its Power
Philosophy of Metaethical Leadership
A leader's moral justification is based on the certainty of his or her knowledge in morality, and such certainty is measured by the size and quality of his or her moral autonomy that affirms that the leader's conscience represents somebody else's ethics. The facts on which people can base their moral justification necessitate behavioral changes among people, and those facts are the evidence that a leader's exercise of his or her authority and power is metaethically valid and sound.

10. Perplexity of Managerial Knowledge
In the Cases of Sales and Marketing Management
Marketing process involve broader range of activities, while sales practices are an essential part of marketing process. Notice the differences in management power and authority exercised in sales and marketing management. However, a concept of moral autonomy or spontaneous management can be equally applied to both practices. Responsibilities of the management in either department are measurable in the same manners when the same principle is applied to make the rules for justifying the management behavior.

11. Philosophy of Risk Assessment
Dimensions of Project Risk and Management Procedures
Risk assessment is a management tool for exposure, admission and disclosure of chances and responsibilities as risks. The risks of a project immediately represent the autonomy of someone who leads the project. A project needs to be evaluated in the terms that the observers of the project can comprehend. Based on the risk elements, a project manager needs to figure out in what categories or dimensions to identify the risks of a project.

12. Managerial Issues in Building Matrix Structures of Organizations
Supplement to Philosophy of Risk Assessment
Justification of a company's performance is given by the outer sources of the company, and responsibilities of the management need to absorb and address the functions and criteria of the audience who observe the company's performance. Increasing the effectiveness of particular organization design reflects the top management's responsibilities, and that in turn represents the adequacy and sufficiency of the management. The logic behind the matrix design of an organization is found in a multi-dimensional analysis of the company's effectiveness.

13. Empowerment: By Design or Default?
Philosophy of Designing Empowerment Programs in Organizations
In employee empowerment, a design needs to be made to re-condition default customs, in which way structures would sustain ideal forms of organizations. It is the balance and the set of priorities between default and design that needs to be addressed. Change management must avoid that the design requires extra modifications and re-designs in the company's exteriors; it must pursue that new visions and values are absorbed in the company's culture and are engaged with the workers, ultimately, by default.

14. On Change Management
The Logic of the Models of Change Management
Managing change is considered the art of balancing the content of change and the participants' acts. Collaborative roles of leadership and management can be utilized to balance the economic modeling and organizational modeling of fundamental change in businesses. By the acts of leadership and management, organizations can adapt to both systemic, structural changes and organizational, cultural changes.

III. Logic and Logistics of Metaethical Business Practices

Introduction to Logic and Logistics of Metaethical Business Practices
If You Have a Problem with Your Spirituality, Fix It before Reading
It is the author's intention to introduce a concept of morality with your confirmation of your own ideas of divinity, regardless of your religion or non-religion. The idea of social responsibility of a business is not complete unless the norms accepted and incorporated in the business is concrete. The discussions of the logic and logistics of metaethical business practices hereinafter extend to the subjects of a society around a business, the environment, nature, and the metaphysics of human conscience.

15. Sound Logic of a New Business
Be Good or Sound Good
To add values to your business, you need to make your logic not only valid but also sound—that is a common rule of business philosophy. Sustainability of your business to its environment is a sign of a sound business. A sound business in a sustainable environment is opted for building, nurturing and curing your community values and wealth. Conducting an impact assessment of your business will help build a better plan for its soundness.

16. Moral Causes in Environmental Disputes
Sound Moral Argument in Environmental Cases
Moral principles and the methods of moral justification need to be simple and clear. Without a simple moral cause and its clear value statement, an argument for sustainable environment can be wasted by either exaggeration of facts or subjective use of interests. Normative measures to moral issues are distinct from legal solutions or financial remedies, and moral principles are the ones to be deduced to another set of principles, but not the ones to be reduced from a higher set of rules.

17. The Art of Communicating Ethical Values in Public
Ethical Business Propositions at Work
A great challenge to businesspeople is being capable of identifying what they offer. The sound logic of being a good salesperson is to state with validity how good is what you offer. Effectively articulating the uniqueness and necessity of your business offering requires that your communication be memorable, believable, and credible.

18. Pseudo Symmetries of Human Factors
Symmetry in Ergonomic Perspective
The final chapter of this book is dedicated to an experiment of how far a business can go to make its propositions metaethically valid and

sound. This chapter is intended to challenge the human factors that instantly accept *de facto* standards as customs, because the concept of such customs do not guarantee the ideas of fairness.

List of Figures and Tables

I

Philosophy of Metaethical Leadership

Introduction to Philosophy of Metaethical Leadership
Causes of Managerial Ethics

When ethics works towards aspiration, so does managerial ethics towards commitment. A company's management styles, assuming they are *ethically* compliant, would involve fair treatment of employees and rewards for ethical conducts. The management must also show sensitivity to the stakeholders, who await the company's action to sustain its commitment to ethical conducts. A company's aspiration requires consistency between policies and actions.

On the other hand, *ethically* compliant behavior of a company may have its own risk: it might hurt the company's effectiveness when it's pattern becomes protective from the company's employees, clients and other stakeholders. Such behavior may also cause harm by abuse when its pattern is built into the company's culture that induces obedience to misused authority, privilege and self-interest of particular set.

Within a frame of social sciences, managerial ethics is measurable by the number of cases that involved violation of, or compliance to, the company's ethical codes. In metaethics, managerial ethics is measurable by the degree of causes that result in aspiration and commitment. However, in metaethics, the method of observation and evaluation must be constantly tested, as well as the process of defining such causes as either ethical or unethical.

In the mind of management, integrating the method of ethical reasoning and behavior is a question of *if* it ever becomes materialized, not *when* it will.

Large or small, any business begins with its owner's, or its founder's, visions and will to bring such ideas to the environment the corporate entity must connect. Daily practices of a company may be controllable at ethically irrelevant level. For example, consider assembling parts into a finished product, stocking the product at the warehouse, taking purchase orders, correctly charging a customer's account, packaging and shipping and delivering products as instructed, and so on. Any of those activities may hardly involve ethical concerns as long as there are no sufficient and necessary reasons to suspect any misconducts engaged in each case. Leaders of a company can lead their workers without asking them to raise moral concerns, if their jobs are instinctively handled, by passing one thing from one place to another. Leaders shall, however, ask their workers to be sensitive enough to some common values, such as kindness, honesty, fairness, devotion, dedication, carefulness, and attention to decency.

For the management, ethics in business is a matter of choice by sufficient and necessary reasoning, and the method of incorporating its own business ethics is essentially a matter of *if*, not *when*. Public or private, a business of any size can thrive and survive over time without any code of ethics to be incorporated, as long as there is no immediate need for it. Ethics becomes crucial and viable, both in principle and in practice, only by choice and at will. It is worthless to argue that business and managerial ethics ought to be the indispensable part of every corporate entity, nor to make a case that ethical behavior in business is vital because it simply can be profitable. On the contrary, it is fundamental to a business that the management be decisive on which part of the business activities must be ethical, or ethically irrelevant otherwise. For any business activities, the choice to make subject matters and contexts ethically relevant is the choice to practice one's knowledge in morality, and such knowledge can be either true or false. Therefore, it is not essential that a business be ethically compliant, but that the agent, who is engaged in such a business, be ethically acquiescent and adequate.

The elementary question is how to acquire and apply a leader's, manager's, and of the company's, ethical values, attitudes and behavior. Managerial challenges in business ethics include creating a process and a procedure for developing managers as moral agents and using their leadership for building an environment in which ethical values are basic to the company's strategy. For such a choice as to make the company's business conducts ethically relevant, what essentially matters is the knowledge that such an action of choice is based on. Both in code and practice, the essence of management responsibility represents the power of knowledge that sustains the company's causes to serve its community. The causes of managerial ethics are measurable by the authenticity of such decision-making knowledge, which makes the company's choice sufficient and necessary, and its moral justification valid and sound.

1. Difference between Authority and Responsibility
In the Context of Managing a Business Structure

Authority is a concept of legitimate knowledge and power in a body that exercises it. Responsibility is a cause to particular behavior in truthfully representing such knowledge and power. Responsibility lies where authority stands. One is held responsible for presenting and representing the knowledge and power one has earned. Depending on whose authority it is to represent, one's responsibility is up to certain level of control. However, since one's responsibility is found in agreement with what authority is, he or she must first have clear understanding of where authority stands, and to what degree an individual or a group can exercise its authority under public contracts. There is a difference in meaning of authority between its philosophical idea and its perceived legitimacy in day-to-day legal and business transactions. Without understanding such differences between philosophical and legal or any other kinds of authority, many entrepreneurs and the top management of corporations may have difficulty in delegating authority to others.

In philosophy, it matters where such an authority stands as the source of true knowledge. The responsibility of a subject that is to obtain such knowledge is the responsibility of representation, or of representing true knowledge. In legal matters as well as in business management, one's responsibility is reduced to a responsibility of presenting already derived or derivative knowledge, as knowledge is granted and located where the associated responsibility is.

Philosophically speaking, authority lies within an individual or a group considered having valid knowledge and legitimate power. Authority is accepted for the benefits derived, which otherwise could not be derived from any other source, and therefore the only individual who has such knowledge and power can exercise it. Responsibility is a concept grounded on such notions that a rational being must perform it as an obligation, without being punishable by neglecting it as a liability, and thus taking responsibility can be subject to reward, honor, and praise. Responsibility is based on the human motives as causes of behavior, is accountable and liable, and hence is a matter that can be conditioned and controlled. A person with responsibility is affected by the control by another source, and one cannot exercise absolute self-control over his or her legitimate power unless one's authority is derived from within.

Reduced in meaning, on the other hand, legal or other non-philosophical authority is the power or right conferred on a person usually by another to act on behalf of somebody else, entailing that authority could be derived from another source. In the meantime, legal responsibility in public contracts includes financial responsibility, integrity, skill, ability, and the likelihood of the agent's faithful conduct and satisfactory work. Here, responsibility under public contracts is regularly subject to control by another source, and one's self-control falls within the boundary of legal authority he or she has.

Comparing philosophical authority and legal or other kinds of authority, there is a difference in how certain it is for an individual with authority to pertain to the true knowledge to be represented. Philosophically, authority entails authenticity of knowledge, and the certainty of knowledge is clearly up to the individual who sees the distinction between acquisition of knowledge and assimilation of it. In public contracts, such knowledge can be approximated in contexts and by conditions. In legal structures, an individual is granted someone else's authority. The certainty of the knowledge, then, acquired or assimilated, is set to a controllable level by another source that granted it. In philosophy, it must be understood that, demonstrating true knowledge is never a matter of one's interpretation of subjects and objects. Authority of knowledge and authenticity of its truth cannot be preached by interpretation, but by recognition and reaffirmation of what actually holds such right and legitimacy as totality. Philosophical authority, therefore, cannot be completely transferable, although it is attainable to a certain level through acquisition and by assimilation. In legal sense, however, since the meaning of authority is reduced to a contextual level, one's authority, already acquired from another source, is measurable up to such controllable level.

Distinction between philosophical and legal responsibility is clear to the extent which one held with responsibility can exercise one's self-control over presenting one's knowledge thus acquired. Since philosophical authority presupposes absolute legitimacy and power in the object of knowledge, one is held primarily responsible for representing such true knowledge. Legal authority sets its boundary of legitimacy and power within the subject of control by another, and one is responsible for presenting one's own knowledge only up to the level that is already reduced and granted.

In the context of managing a business or managing the structure of an organization, overall or partial, one's intensity of authority and responsibility falls within the plane of legal content under public contracts. Therefore, one's authority is approximated and assimilated from another source, and one's responsibility is limited to the truthful level and certainty of such knowledge acquired as a conditional, provisional, and qualified authority. Understanding the differences between philosophical and legal authority, entrepreneurs and top managers may consider what level of responsibility they should grant by delegation. In order to remain in control over the delegated, the authority needs to be set with the limitations to the responsibility of the delegated. The authority of the delegated body, therefore, has a characteristic of what contexts and causes it consists of, and the responsibility of representing them has limited liabilities by design. Confusion of legal authority with one's absolute, philosophical authority may produce a poor controller of such causes within an organization.

Entrepreneurs and upper-level managers must deal with these delegation processes in an attempt to make the transition from the company's entrepreneurial or pre-expansion stage to overall professional management. Delegation of responsibility and the implementation of formal controls are the key steps in making such a transition. The question is how much those top managers can give up their authority to engage lower-class managers with their own responsibilities for representing newly claimed power bases.

In order to fight poor motivation and lack of commitment, business owners have a challenge in changing their management style and redirecting the structure of a company. By giving up their own authority and getting employees to take full responsibility for whatever decisions made in conditions of production, personnel, quality control, and/or share or sales growth, the owners have chances in raising performance standards and increasing the company's competence.

Entrepreneurs are often careless administrators, expressing their enthusiasm for expanding businesses with their own might. To cope with the proper administrative controls in place, entrepreneurs need to hire capable managers, give them authority and responsibility, and consult with them regularly. Few entrepreneurs easily give up authority and responsibility. It is understood that, however, their businesses can profit, if they concentrate their own efforts on the tasks they do best and delegate other functions to managers best suited for them by disposition and discipline.

In larger organizations, there can be found the plight of middle managers that have their boss's responsibility without the boss's authority. Middle managers function as specialists and generalists at the same time, and they meet the conflicting demands of superiors, subordinates, and peers. Although middle management positions are increasingly common in many divisionalized organizations, their roles and responsibilities are often misunderstood. Their job requirements must state clearly in what context and condition the middle management can exercise their own authority.

Like many managers in the middle, employees also regularly find themselves in situations where they have responsibility but not authority to get things done. They have a challenge in leading when they are not the real bosses. To exercise lateral leadership of middle managers, they need to have certain level of authority as informal power, which allows a person to lead a group regardless of his or her formal role. They need their own system of setting objectives and engaging other participants with the use of effective feedback.

Upper-level managers often fail to realize the difficulties of first-level or middle managers that are positioned among employees. Successful first-level and middle supervisors need to establish their identity with certain informal authority that produces interpersonal influence, and their formal responsibility associated with it. It is the responsibility of upper management to recognize the difficulties associated with the position and help lower-class supervisors develop their power bases.

Many business experts urge executives of companies to delegate their responsibility. However well meaning, the distributors of such advice usually underestimate the difficulty, which entrepreneurs and top managers have in giving up their cherished privileges. Entrepreneurs pride themselves of possessing their knowledge and skill, and often thrive to be in all places at once. Top managers are inclined to securing their benefits derived from their hard-earned authority. However, as their organizations expand, their staffs can never mature without delegation of such knowledge and power, and they would not have the capability to map the company's courses of action.

Delegation of authority needs to take place in an organization, segment by segment. A company needs to execute a management strategy in a decentralized manner, in order to achieve high growth rates in each segment through a process of transformation. Responsibilities must be understood with the fact that the matching authority exists, whereas the authority of each segment can vary by context and condition. Delegation of authority needs to be understood by how formal the delegated authority is to the extent of its authenticity, and needs to be performed in agreement with what content it must be transferred. May such understanding help managers realize clear responsibilities for their representation and exercise of their granted knowledge and power.

2. On Definition of Business Ethics
Understanding of Authority and Responsibility

Concepts of ethics necessitate a set of standards by which a group or community decides to regulate its behavior, distinguishably as what is legitimate and acceptable in pursuit of one's aims. Ethics as customized can be understood as such a set of standards by definition. Use of ethics may not be necessarily associated with all aspects of life or activities, and hence it makes sense to discuss it within a restricted area or in reduced sense. In many cases, such as medical, legal, and business ethics, all the use of ethics concerns its derived legitimacy and tolerance as particular set of standards in certain contexts. In practice, we need to decide what types of moral standards are applicable to particular interests of our lives. In like manners, business ethics is bound by the needs of the groups and individuals engaged in particular business region of our social system.

Subject Matters in Business Ethics

How can we, then, define the clear standards of business ethics? The more business ethics secures its status in organizations across the society, the more confusing it appears to their managers and their constituencies as to what standard actually deserves such an anchoring status as a solid ground rule. As far as the nature of moral justification is concerned, few business ethicists have offered their community the practical advice they need, simply because the standards they proclaim are always in context. Conflicting factors involves not that business people dislike the idea of doing the right thing, but whose interests and needs are to be considered first, or most relevant, and the potential costs of planning and implementing such standards of doing the right thing.

There is a clash of ideas in business ethics and management decision-making, when a company's business cases involve formulating a corporate response to the incidents that happen, to the communities that are affected, and to government agencies and other corporate stakeholders that are engaged. There are also disagreements among those who make decisions over what preventive measures to use and how the company and its employees can be the agents of such ethical standards. These details influence how the top managers define the company's ethical standards in conducting a business, for which more refined logic or system of moral justification becomes crucial.

It might be a common belief that there are some single, general approaches to business ethics. In reality, however, the search for a grand, unifying principle of management morality often leads to frustration and doubt. The moral dilemmas that many managers face are, in essence, clashes among different spheres of responsibility. In a framework for resolving ethical issues, managers' responsibilities—to shareholders, employees, other stakeholder groups, and to their own values and commitments in life—conflict with each other. The framework needs to be analyzed in terms of the practicality of duties, consequences, and personal values. Therefore, we need to have an analytic framework for setting a course of ethical conduct and the element of business ethics, which brings together basic considerations in moral philosophy with realistic pressures, perspectives, and concerns of business executives.

Many established approaches, such as stakeholder analysis, equity theory, goal-based, and anything else that a system of ethical thinking needs to be based on, would simply come short of comparing the parities or disparities of influence and power among the members of a diverse business community. Even with a good intention of the management to do no harm to any people or groups, the management still needs to take cases one at a time.

Redefining Business Ethics of Corporations

Here, the clear understanding and differentiation of authority and responsibility that each moral agent holds in every situation, must be the starting point of defining business ethics. Ethical rules can be based on the differences made in a description of responsibilities that each authority in particular terms and conditions would have. Whether one's responsibility is described as his or her duty, right, or a goal, the very description of responsibility itself helps redefine the authority in concern. Then, we can start analyzing which responsibility would apply to particular set of constituency, stakeholders as well as customers and suppliers, all of which could be either at present, unreachable, simply invisible behind the scene, or even apparently unthinkable to be related to the business in concern.

The definition of business ethics begins with defining the responsibilities of those who engage in particular aspects of business; based on the knowledge of what authority they have, and based on where such accounts of knowledge can be located, with responsibilities, or lack thereof. As the next step, link the statement of such responsibilities and knowledge, both the source of knowledge and the knowledge base, to the constituency to be engaged, as an object, with the business activities in concern. Then draw the line and pick the morally relevant part of the business responsibilities, and list them, in form of a map or matrices.

Now in such a matrix of descriptions we would see the causal relationships among all those who engage in one big circle and cycle of a business. We can then separate the issues, by sorting the list by context, significance (or potential risk) and decision level. Reformatting such lists of moral relations would make a detailed analysis of a company's ethical conducts, and hence by subject this would make a statement of ethical standards. A company's business ethics is redefined as a concentrate of such coordinated sets of standards across the board.

3. On Leadership and Ethics
Can Managers Be Good Leaders with or without Ethics?

If moral issues were to be solved by using one's own judgment based on what we call common sense, then there would be actually no apparently serious ethics issues around. Real moral issues in a business environment arise when someone's decision-making becomes complicated and difficult because of two or more conflicting interests that would give him or her several different options to choose from. A quandary of this sort is an ethical dilemma; depending on whom the decision may affect, only particular groups of people would benefit from one's decision, while other constituents may not. Certain logic or reasoning may sound right because it benefits some people, while it may not make sense to others because it does not appeal to their own ethics.

Morality in business is sometimes a subject matter, but it also depends on the context of dealing. Use of ethics in business is subjective as far as the achievement of particular goal is concerned. One's business ethics is also subject to change accordingly when different types of jobs, occupations, people and situations are concerned. If moneymaking or profit maximization is a single, virtue-like goal to achieve, where can we find any use of morality, besides legality of the matters in concern? If one's goal is set to controlling production and service quality, how much does the quality of one's ethics matter? If the matter in concern is simply to get things done, how can we relate our ethics to productivity?

Answer may be in the mode of '*it depends*,' because we need to specify the interests and objectives of a group involved.

Can leaders and managers be good at maximum achievement of goals, with or without ethics? If the goal is morally relevant, leaders and managers must be adequate when using their ethics. The question needs to be addressed in two different ways. If a question is *how* to be good, it is the question of *how* to determine each matter or case in its relevance to morality, and if a question is *what* kind of leaders and managers are to be considered adequate, the question is *what* sort of ultimate concern one's ethics must address. For leaders and managers, to be good *without* ethics, there would be no question about any ethicalness of dealing such a subject or situation; to be good *with* the use of ethics, they need to be ethically competent themselves so that they can represent others ideas of morality. The former is a practical concern of skills and tactics; the latter is a personal quest of knowledge and discipline. To ethically succeed in business, one must take courses of action in both ways.

Overall, in all subject matters and contexts, there needs to be a set of guidelines for leaders and managers who want to be *good*. Such guidelines are necessary so that the definition of *good* is by any means concrete but variant. Whether the goal is to maximize profit or to save someone's life, a leader or manager's decision and the action with the use of ethics must be based on the fact that the decision maker's value is intrinsically good. Both moneymaking and saving someone's life are intrinsically good as long as the achievement of either would benefit someone; achieving such a state can be justifiable even if it costs someone else's loss, money or life. Any loss of money or life would be understood with moral support, if the decision for it were to be just. Such moral justification may be possible only with the concrete definition of one's moral autonomy, which may seem philosophically impossible.

What sort of judgment would it be, then, if success in business were intrinsically good no matter what and in any context? A decision is either morally justifiable, or it is acceptable when it is morally irrelevant. The former is good for leaders and managers *with* ethics; the latter is good *without* ethics. Some business and management issues are apparently both morally relevant to some people and not so to others; therefore, the action to distinguish the moral relevance of a matter or a case needs to be based on thorough research of facts. Moral good cannot be attained without being ethical; on the other hand, ethics should not be brought up when the issue is morally irrelevant. The decision-making in whether to use ethics for certain matter or particular case must be logically valid and sound.

To answer all the questions related to such an ethical dilemma in business, one must define the legitimacy of one's moral concerns, *i.e.*, at what point one must raise his or her own moral concerns that would be everybody else's business. Defining and refining such a resolution would be a big agenda for one's ethical succession, personally and individually, but when it comes down to business, one could also consider a quick setup for an environment where he or she *does not* need to raise ethical concerns, nor to exercise one's hard-earned ethics. To do things at morally irrelevant level, one must find a safe harbor for others' moral affairs, but that is not by lowering one's ethical standards but by simply developing a system that provides others with their job descriptions and their standard procedures in a morally free zone. Once such an environment was made, good leaders and managers would have no need to carry around the code of ethics all the time.

4. Moral Use of Autonomy and Power
Philosophy of Metaethical Leadership

Meaning of *power* presupposes an *authoritative* supremacy that is used in order to cease an opportunity and make something possible. Since in physical sense power is the rate at which certain mechanical work is done or at which energy is spent, it concerns the direction to which energy is imposed, which in either way can be repressive or productive. Any physical direction of power deals with the degree to which something is bound for certain direction, and as long as the law of physics conserves the total energy, such a motion or momentum may not be relevant to human will to articulate any qualitative change that would add the value of either positive or negative interpretation. It is unclear if we can evaluate such positive or negative tones of power only by using the existing physical measures, and such classifications of power and its directions would leave us in business with some unresolved questions such as in what sense (or in what way) power is determined repressive or productive.

If such a determination or an interpretation is solely dependable on the motive of a person who causes change in something, it may only result in a conflict of interests among those who will be affected by such a change. Some may call it oppressive or tyrannical; others may appreciate it as creative, useful, and thus acceptable. Such a conflict may be resolved in social context by majority rule, or could remain undecided if it is just the matter of art (that some people get but some do not). If the issue is totally up to one's aesthetic interpretation, any argument is reduced to a mere opinion, and in such a way, anyone's moral justification reflects only the values of the agent who makes judgment.

Such indecisiveness of a direction of power in human condition may necessitate reconstructing a proper measure of change made by an exercise of power. It is the scale of power forced by some legitimate *authority*, but what kind of authority would it be? Authority can be either acceptable for its derived benefits, which is positive and productive, or regarded as oppressive and repressive by the opponents of such authority. If the authority is merely political or legal, it never exceeds the social or personal limitations in defining what is legitimate and is subject to change over time. If a direction of power pertains to moral authority, however, an exercise of power is necessarily productive.

The power exercised in moral sense is the power of aspiration that is to strive to guide, and its ultimate goal is to direct a knower what is moral as factual knowledge. Moral belief, moral thought, and *moral justification* are the expressions and practices of such knowledge. Such expressions are developed or produced in a direction to which power is properly exercised. Ethics is a study of morality, and ethics is used in order to measure the exercise of power. By establishing a set of ethical standards, power used in any given expression or operation can be evaluated how ethical the exercise of power is. Such moral scales are set to evaluate an exercise of power based on different standards, from one's personal ethical standpoints to normative ones, up to the ultimate knowledge of morality.

Such a study in the development and classification of morality is *metaethics*, and in metaethics, morality is pursued as the ultimate goal of obtaining knowledge that is not just relative to those who interpret it, but is valid and sound regardless of its subject matter or context. In logic, the validity and soundness of such knowledge are analyzed in two different modes: *de dicto* moral claim (that is necessarily true to a whole assertion of a subject matter) and *de re* claim (that is necessarily true in particular context). The distinction between those two modes has long troubled those who were in attempt to reconcile them. That attempt itself becomes a purpose of metaethics, and after constructing a unifying axiom for both *de dicto* and *de re* states of morality, there can be proper standards set forth to measure the use of power to cause change in the right direction.

Consider a two-dimensional system for such *de dicto* and *de re* classifications of morality, construct the third dimension as the magnitude of exercising the power to cause changes in one's moral behavior. In addition to a time scale, a proper measure for the right use of power forms another dimension, as the product of existing three-dimensional system of *de dicto* and *de re* morality and their cause. Such a power measure can be set as moral dimension that extends personal ethics to ultimate knowledge of moral authority. Here we will have a five-dimensional universe to evaluate a use of power in accordance with its level of moral autonomy.

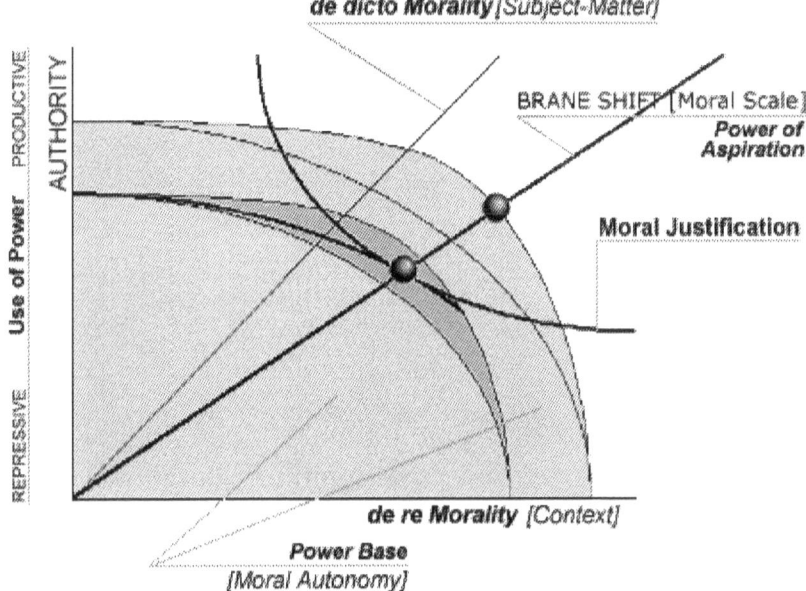

Figure 1. Moral Use of Authority and Its Power

Use of power is productive to the extent that the moral authority is represented and exercised in a legitimate way. The legitimacy of the use of power is measured by the moral autonomy that the agent of power represents. The moral autonomy, in its size and quality, is the power base of an agent, who governs, leads or manages an entity, and in a business entity, that power base represents the quality of a leader, whose moral justification must be based on the certitude of his or her knowledge in what is right.

Our act of moral justification may have a serious flaw when it is based merely on our own values. Justification can be a flawed judgment when it is based not on facts but on values, unless such values are everybody else's facts—to say the *most*. A leader's moral justification is based on the certainty of his or her knowledge in morality, and such certainty is measured by the size and quality of his or her moral autonomy that affirms that the leader's conscience represents somebody else's ethics. It is not a leader's values that essentially affect people's behavior in metaethics. The facts on which people can base their moral justification necessitate behavioral changes among people, and those facts are the evidence that a leader's exercise of his or her authority and power is metaethically valid and sound.

5. Lead Where Workers' Morals Don't Collide

How to Let Workers Deal with Others Effectively

To make ethics work in business, it is sometimes proper not telling employees what a virtue is. In everyday business that *sometimes* mean a long period of time, almost all the time of working hours when the workers are to deal with numerous personalities of others. Ethical managers need to follow a simple step to make their ethics work: keep workers away from unnecessary moral inquiries.

Let your workers not raise moral questions against the leader or about the business policy, unless the leader him or herself is in fact in charge of such matters as a corporate moral officer, ombud, or any of such sorts.

Among those highly respected corporate leaders, few things are common regarding their personality and individuality, or in other words, who they are and what they are. However, it is still possible to characterize and even theorize how those leaders can behave in commonly acceptable manners. Here is a sample that everyone could follow. A highly skilled and conceivably good manager is someone who is able to say two things one after another that every worker can heed: '*Don't even think about it; just do it*' and, '*Use your judgment.*'

Even as they may appear conflicting, these are two primary statements about what workers are supposed to do. A leader with skills can manage everyday business situations, internal or external, within a moral domain shared by both the leader and workers. This does not necessarily mean that the leader is *prima facie* moral, nor he or she is indeed a spiritual leader in a sense that he or she commits no sin. Instead, any leader who can control his or her domain of autonomy is the one who holds the leash on workers who otherwise might put their own sense of morality in practice.

The best scenario in managing an organization can be the one in which no one raises ethical questions because they have no need to do so. Most employees would value their work environment where many different working styles are nurtured. Meanwhile, however, not so many experienced and matured workers are able to get along with the company's new policy or system if they find them uneasy to fit in. A good manager is the one who can create an environment which workers can fit in, without moral objections. Creating a change causes more moral concerns rather than mere anxieties about job security. Fear is the enemy of logic, and a manager doesn't want his or her workers go awry by emotion and fear that the result and consequence might fall out of the logical scheme of management. One unified moral environment may be out of reach for many, but for those who consider themselves ordinary managers, it is necessary to clear the fear of moral inquiries, by creating an environment where there is no urge for workers to bring up any of such questions.

Let them not confuse technicality with morality, that is, level off workers' duties at which their techniques can fix. Where workers can manage their tasks within their autonomy, most work issues are just the matter of technicality that can be resolved by acquiring particular technical skills and knowledge. On the other hand, in order to prevent corruptions among workers, a good manager needs to limit workers' duties at morally irrelevant level. Let no workers put their morality into action, unless they can be fully trusted, or otherwise a manager by him or herself has a chance to set a perfect example of handling such a situation.

A moral worker can handle a situation by deciding which side has an ample moral claim and by reaching a common ground as to agree on how the situation be handled. An ordinary worker without such skills needs to be advised to follow a manual that requires the worker to say just few words about the company's policy, unless he or she is considered capable of making an exception in the right way. Workers need to make their customers understand the company's policy, as the customer's claim needs to be addressed at the same time. Business requires norms and a worker should not put his or her moral values in the first place, unless his or her ethical concerns are the common awareness of the many. Those ethical concerns need to be dealt with mutual understanding and compassion followed by certain action, and in business, such an action can be taken as instructed, so that the leader's moral autonomy covers and represents the worker's ethical concerns. In short, a worker's contextual ethics can be maintained if they are allowed to deal with such concerns that are defined as technical matters. The worker's once ethical concerns are no longer the matter of '*don't do it*' but the matter of '*just do it.*'

Good leaders' idea of technicality corresponds with their practices of 'just doing' and 'making judgment' by workers. Workers need not to think about moral questions when things can be done technically and making judgment is not about making a moral decision. To prevent moral questions against their boss, the leader needs to keep the workers away from either making projection of their personal values or instant discounting of an ideal of what is right. To make things in everyday business morally irrelevant, the manager needs to set up a working environment where workers find no moral issues around. Wise workers might make it possible by themselves not introducing their self-righteousness, but most workers need guidance from their leaders.

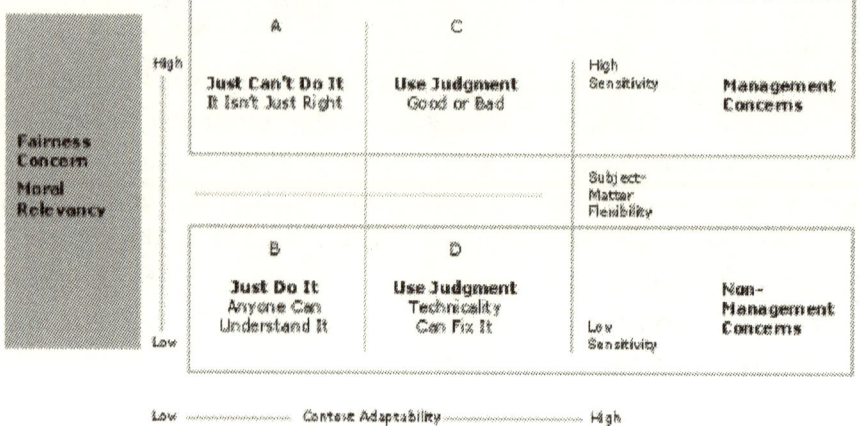

Figure 2. Moral Relevance of Decision-Making

6. Moral Relevance of Diversity Management
Unity and Diversity Concerns in Decision-Making

Sustaining diversity in a society and workplace often encounters a conflict with the very interests of the different groups, when they push too hard their own set of norms. It is a conflict of interests in the reasonable dealing of a diversified entity. However, not necessarily such a conflict is the clash of moral values; it is a call for moral arguments in favor of advancing one set of values over the other. That way, a moral argument is conveniently used, misused, and abused.

Sound moral arguments entail imperatives to equitable treatment of participants, based on the good worth of mutual respect and togetherness in a diverse society, and more critically, toward the higher merit of sharing the common good in a unified society. If anything falls short of perceived values of respect, however, such an incident or a condition may immediately declared as discrimination. Discrimination can be used as a voucher for boosting one group's standing through re-compensation, retaliation, and retribution. Such counter action often goes beyond the necessity for amendment and reconciliation.

For many, diversity is the rhetoric for fairness, based on vague belief in the positive impact on the society's functioning, supported by quite psychological but not always material development in the profit measurement, *i.e.*, enhanced productivity, improved marketability, increased effectiveness, and so on. When the society's functioning of diversity fails, there awaits a rigid application of dogmatic principles against discrimination. It is confusing when the core values of diversity concerns are endangered by the false accusation of discrimination, while discrimination *is* a necessary condition in favor of diversification. It is confusing when we associate moral argument directly with diversification and start accusing its fundamental social condition, discrimination, by denouncing differentiation in always-negative sense. Worse, both executives and working-class tend to realize that they can merely rely on their subjective or inter-subjective sensitivity in decision-making, which is far below the state of morality where common sense and good judgment make way for the absolute; many people are not even sure whose common sense is in concern when diversity is at stake.

Moral Argument in Decision-Making

It is crucial not to confuse morality with technicality, and more importantly, fairness with diversity. Diversity is a function that follows the form of fairness, or unity, which is the ultimate concern of humanity. Diversity is a function in practice that concerns togetherness in understanding differences. Diversity is *not* reconciliation to share the common good as one, which *is* the unity concern, a step further in a society toward the essential state of humanity. Many moral arguments will fail without such a clear distinction between unity and diversity, or between form and function, if they claim morality as the first principle regardless of which state is in concern. Unity concerns are moral by definition; diversity concerns are somewhat morally relevant but they merely sustain non-essential human benefit in which making choices is not always the matter of ethics. Choosing between competing sets is not, and shall not be a direct objective of self-interest, because it is not always morally relevant. It is crucial, then, to know what case, how and why such a case, is morally relevant.

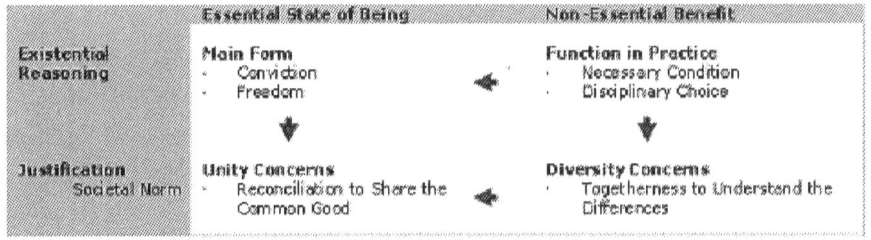

Adapted from Table 4. Individual Reason of Existence and Unity Concerns in Society
A Book of Metaethics, Andrew Minase, 2001, ISBN 0595144675, Chapter 17, p. 146

Table 1. Distinction between Form of Unity and Function of Diversity

Categorical Imperative of Choice in Decision-Making

Managing diversity does not necessarily presuppose management's moral conscience in the first order. Moral imperative in decision-making is a dependent variable to the moral relevancy of the very case, subject-mater or context in concern. The urge for moral argument in managing diversity can be merely based on the presumption that discrimination is by any means wrong. Such a notion, many believe that, would necessitate certain positive impact on sustaining diversity in return for eliminating discriminatory arrangements as a symptom of mismanagement. That type of notion is self-contradictory, when the distinction between discrimination and differentiation is highly subjective and biased. Diversification is possible because of differentiation, which may only be morally relevant to certain degree. It is proactive understanding of differences between the sets of values that sustain the notion of diversity. Discrimination is no blow to the entities of different value sets as long as the purpose of differentiation is just. Providing diverse standards and trying different approaches can be done by means of accessibility and equal opportunity. It is also a matter of perception whether particular conduct is labeled as discrimination, which is reciprocal to the intention of establishing equity. When management has difficulty in producing compelling evidence to equity based on the diverse series of achievements, the opponents of discrimination may observe the same situation as inequity, and may bring their own version of inequity, discrimination, alienation and isolation of others. Then any moral argument used within the concept of diversity may lose its relevancy if its use is constrained to self-interest, a matter of preference and choice. Choice is ever-present in decision-making, but is not what immediately needs to be damned; it is the motive of making such a choice that is to be argued in accordance with its relevance to morality.

More humanly speaking, diversity among groups and people is not in essence a moral imperative, but morally relevant by subject and in context to the extent of how much ethical values must be taken into considerations when making appropriate choices. Moral claims against any types of differentiated plans, by holding a notion that everything must be equal to be fair, are illogical, because such claims discount the very distinction between unity and diversity, the notion's precondition. The concern for unity requires fairness in its pure form. If we diversify, differences must be given priorities, and making choices among such differences must be permitted but controlled and modified. Moral argument must first be independent from the social order that can be either unified or diversified, to which different sets of ethics must be applied accordingly.

Relevance of Ethics in Decision-Making

In a decision-making model, ethics needs to be applied in accordance with its relevancy. Morality does not necessarily pose significance in many actions taken in a daily business. However, the conscience matters when it tells in what case ethical decision-making be commended; you shall not say 'it does not matter' unless you know for sure it doesn't. The following plans would help management and working class alike distinguish which case is in concern when applying one's ethics as the society's norm.

There is a striking difference in the perceived responsibility between management and working class when it comes to decision-making. Higher sensitivity to ethical conduct and flexibility to the subject matter in concern may attach to management responsibility, while workers may be given some activates of lesser moral sensitivity.

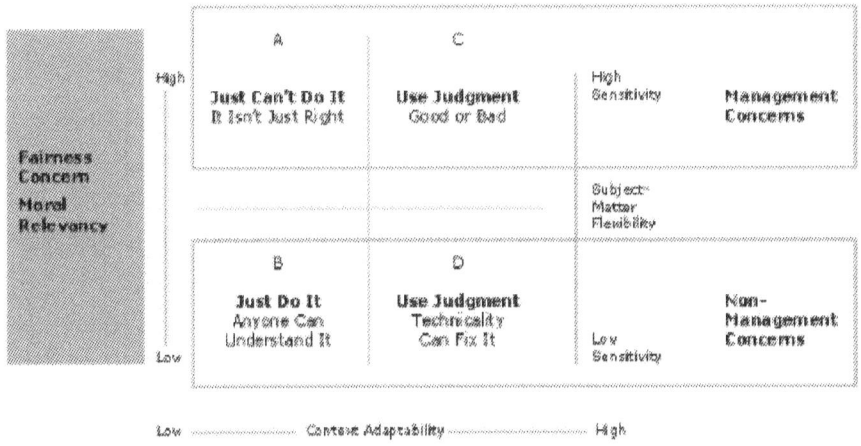

Figure 2. Moral Relevance of Decision-Making

Meanwhile, the applicability of both managers' and workers' conduct also needs to be discussed in order for such a conduct to be commended in many contexts—occasions, professions, and individuals alike. Decision-making is morally relevant in context, and if its taken out of context, it must be always appropriate, and acceptable regardless of the case in concern. In addition, not all conducts in decision-making are morally relevant to certain degree; some are highly, others hardly. While life and death situation is an important subject matter in decision-making, such a conduct may be persistent in a case of physician but may not in a situation like the physician punching a time card, although even that should be done right, to some extent.

With such distinctions between the pre-conditioned collective states (unity and diversity) and among the particular cases of conduct (subject matter and context) to which morality and thus ethical concerns are to be relevant, let be introduced an integrated framework of making choices, in relevance to the ethical behavior of decision-making.

Framework of Managing Unity and Diversity

Dynamics of Ethical Choice

Integrity of decision-making lies on what ground an ethical conduct is to be managed. To know what ground is the case in concern, both management and working-class of the society need to have a model pattern of behavior, against which particular conduct is to be measured and warranted. The distinction between the form of unity and the function(s) of diversity is to be classified as the categorical moral imperative and its significance of moral relevance. The differences among the subject matters and contexts of particular behavior are plotted and scattered across the coordinate system of moral sensitivity and moral adaptability. The diagram herein conceived would show in what case someone must use ethics to certain extent, and would explain what type(s) of action would be expected in a person in particular society or company.

To make certain conduct in decision-making measurable, we may attach some tangible and perceivable effects to the functioning of the system in development. Attach productivity scale as the result of significance in moral relevance, to the axis where the outcome of particular conduct, or the cause level, is to be measured. With assumptions and adjustments, here we predict certain area of conduct and its result as relatively low in its relevance to morality, and thus harmless; call it a risk-free zone or whatever, only with certain degree of accuracy.

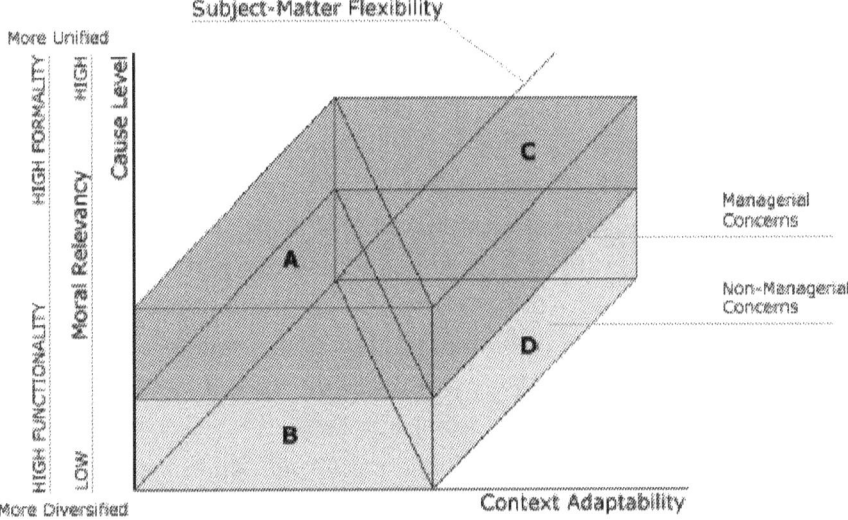

Figure 3. Making Ethical Choice in Action [Base Diagram]

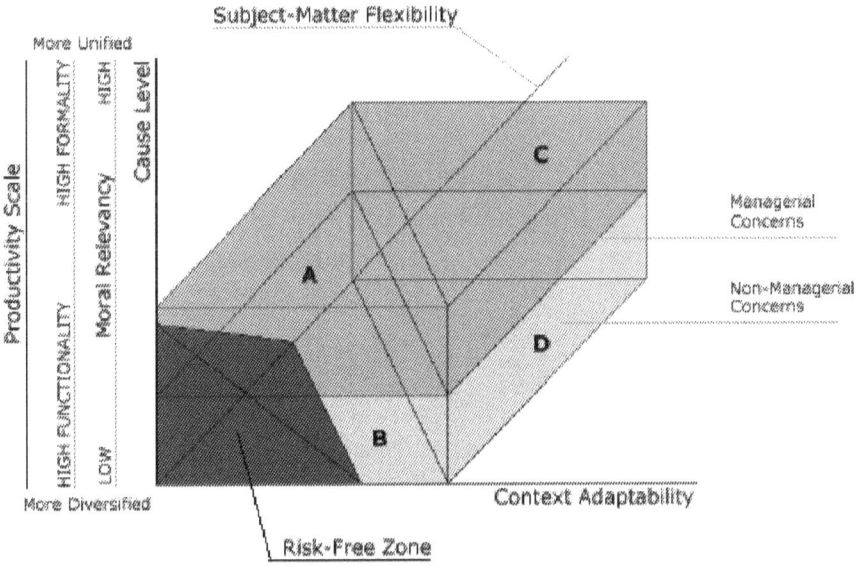

Figure 4. Measuring Ethical Choice in Action

Revisiting Moral Justification of Decision-Making

Be cautious, however, because development of such value systems and analyses by use of them would be merely approximate as to what conduct in any given case is in fact justifiable. A human society has its own limits to decide particular conduct is just, without the concrete knowledge of what conduct is in demand. The interceding spirit of justice and the force of justification may only be approximated and represented within a domain of human imagination and action. As for a smaller group of people, such as a business entity, the realm of its functioning in the state of ethical affairs would be far less momentous, sometimes hardly up to its societal demand of justice and expectation of fairness. Here, a society's or a company's supply of justifiable behavior and its domain of sound functioning need to be enhanced in order to meet such demand. This enhancement, adjustment or improvement of its course of action, may be scientifically observed in a shift of a supply curve and/or the shift of entire brane that surfaces the outreaching points of the entity's behavioral domain. It is a pattern of ethical succession of particular entity, a society or a company, with a discerning mind of what needs to be done right, or at least, what just needs to be done without questioning one's motives behind making any choices.

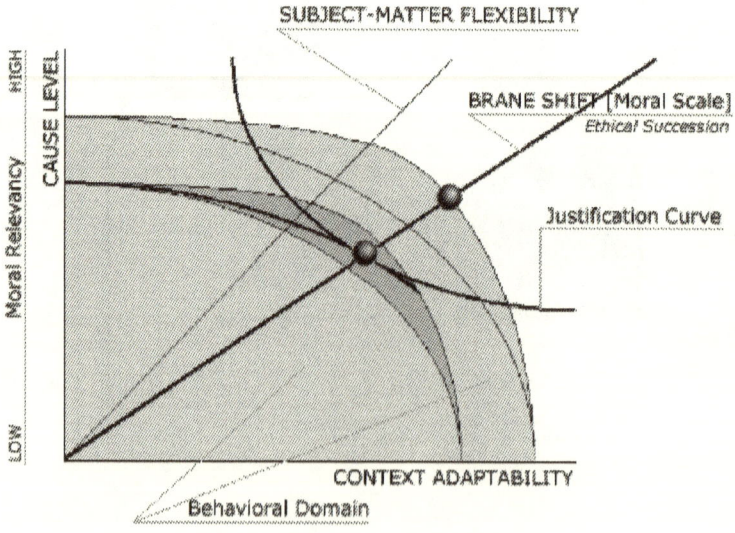

Figure 5. Moral Justification and Ethical Succession

7. Metaethical Judgment in a Nutshell

Sensitivity to the Fact, the Constituency, and the Absolute

In study of ethics, applying ethics is by itself indeed a moral challenge. Where moral principles are strict and way above our day-to-day living standards, it is hard to define a convincing moral outlook on a matter of fact that is too common to our own sense and sensitivity. If we first struggle to find answers in the abstract, we fail to recognize what they are. Based on our blurred understanding of what principles are, we force ourselves to analyze how it is possible that we make moral justification.

To make their judgment ethical, most people in a managerial position would learn to keep their sensitivity high, the sense that would help recognize the differences in values. This is what you would learn in school where you are allowed to study without finding absolutely right or wrong answers. The questions in people's moral concerns are: how we can judge what we are doing is right, under what circumstance, to what extent, *etc.*—a pile of how-to questions without attaining a clear understanding of what is. Applying ethics needs to begin with what our sensitivity is, where and whom it needs to be addressed or targeted, and when, if applicable, ever before discussing how.

Applying *our* sensitivity to what it matters begins with learning what basic components we need to conduct our logical analysis of how we apply our judgment. First, it is crucial to collect all the information we need to understand, such as the following:

Basic Information:
[0] Absolute measure: ultimate concern before the fact to be known,
[1] Value of the fact in concern: how much it is worth,
[2] Observers of the fact: who will be involved in a decision and an action to witness the fact.

What really matters in making judgment is our *sensitivity* to the *fact*, to the *constituency*, and to the *absolute*. Value of the fact is the magnitude of particular fact that would matter to somebody; that somebody needs to be involved as our constituency; then we still need to know what would matter to all of them in the first place, no matter what particular fact may turn out to be. If our concern is the ultimate peace to the entire world, then, no matter how we obtained information that someone is about to launch an earth-sized atomic bomb, we may have to stand up and tell the world, even though some of the world would benefit from such a terror.

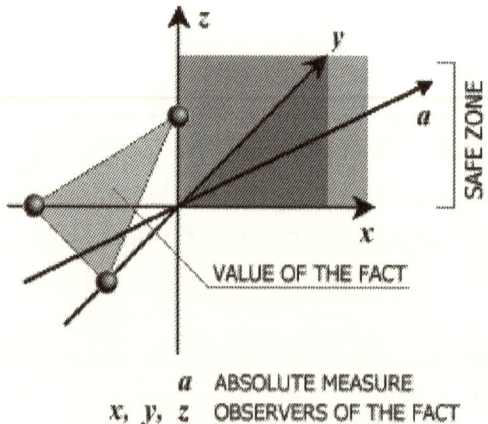

a   ABSOLUTE MEASURE
x, *y*, *z*   OBSERVERS OF THE FACT

Figure 6. System of Value Judgment

Yet, we would not know whether such an act is indeed a kind of terrorism unless we know who really presses the button. Then we will need to answer back to what our absolute measure was: was it a blessing of the sky, or a projection of our own values? The absolute measure of concern will help us shift the entire coordinate system to certain direction so that all the quadrants moves into a safe zone.

Such a mechanism can be drawn into a conceivable picture that makes it simple to analyze our judgment. Value of the fact is to be located by the coordinates with respect to some set of reference. As for coordinates, we would assemble a board meeting of at least three parties in concern: the first party, his or her immediate object, and bystanders or witnesses who may be affected by the relationship between the first two parties. The interests of the first two parties need to be prioritized to initiate an operation. The first party is the party to whom the fact in concern affects in the first place. A geometric form of this fact-value analysis looks like the one shown in the above picture.

Such a system is used to analyze some tricky questions to our day-to-day concerns, such as the following:

Question 1:
How can we make moral justification based on the information that has been disclosed to us, without knowing whether such information is confidential and privileged; under what circumstance is it right to tell others about such information?

Question 2:
How can we make moral justification to develop personal relationships with someone in a close environment, such as workplace; under what circumstance can we go for such an interpersonal affairs that may or may not have some unexpected consequences to somebody else?

The question is answered by constructing the following scenarios:

Basic Information for Question 1:

[0] Absolute measure: ultimate concern before the fact to be known [*e.g.* someone set a bomb],

[1] Value of the fact a judgment is based upon: how much it matters, positive or negative,

[2] Source and target of the disclosure: source of the original information, who else to be involved.

Coordinate System for Question 1:

x: Source of the disclosure [or the first party]

y: Primary recipient of the information [or the second party]

z: Bystander(s) [third party]

Note: The source of disclosure may or may not be the person who owns the information; it might come from somebody else. Recipient may not be always the first party it could be a bystander. Change the axis accordingly, based on where the *information* is located.

Basic Information for Question 2:

[0] Absolute measure: ultimate concern before the fact to be known [*e.g.* you found a soul mate],

[1] Value of the relationship: how hot it is [to you, to him or her, and to somebody else],

[2] Who is involved in the affair: how each one perceives it, how it affects morale or job performance.

Coordinate System for Question 2:

x: Source of the passion [the person attracted to particular someone]

y: Primary target of the passion [that particular someone]

z: Bystander(s) [other(s) in the work (or social) environment]

Note: If the system is made for a relationship between two parties, then the first two coordinates (x, y) should represent those two bodies, depending on who initiated the relationship. We can also use this system to analyze how much other people in a workplace are affected, based on the affair of the first two parties.

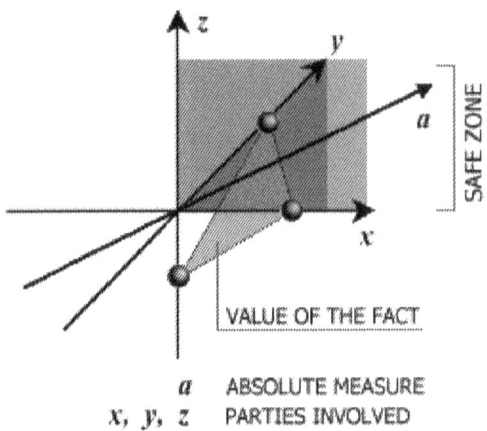

Figure 7. System of Value Judgment in a Safe Zone

For the matter of convenience, first, find the *safe zone* of the coordinate system. If each value of the fact falls in the safe zone, we could go for *it*, whatever it might be. Second, however, ask repeatedly what absolute measure of sensitivity we use; and *that* should be taken into consideration in the first place. Even though the disclosure of some information may negatively affect somebody in concern for the time being, if the ultimate concern is to save the whole world [all the constituency] from some unfortunate consequence to all of them, then the absolute measure should hold no matter what the fact is. The measure shifts all the quadrants to the safe zone.

As for the Question 1, the first party's sensitivity is directed to all the plots behind the scene and all the strings attached to the propositions made to someone who received the information. The information to be disclosed may or may not be confidential, because somebody else beside the two primary parties may have already known it.

As the matter of fact, however, it may not concern us whether it is privileged or not. Remember, this is *not* a cross section analysis. This is to analyze how it affects once all the people in concern were informed of certain fact. It is *not* the matter of when, because our judgment is used once and for all. This analysis is *not* to question whether a disclosure is ethical or not; the value of our judgment is based on the value of the fact we know, and the question is how to tell somebody about it.

If we see that telling others about someone or something is *unsafe*, we need to determine which matter to move first. To whom the information is to be transferred, to what extent, so that one variable may fall into a safe zone; then second, what to move next, and so on. In the meantime, we need to have a guiding star to what we are doing: we need to save all others, not just ourselves, from unbearable consequences. Therefore, we always need to question where the star is, and whether that is what we look for. When we become such a star and set an example, we must make sure that everybody knows what the lesson would be.

Leave the question of what *passion* really is, for now, to answer the Question 2. Although we may take the interests of the two parties in an affair in the first place, when we think of a consequence, we need to consider how it might affect others as well, the group of the third party. The affair may affect their morale, work ethics, resulting in a decrease in their job performance.

Answer to the Question 2 is to find where to draw the line. The system may look complicate, but the order is simple: where the line is. If all the values of the affair are found in a safe zone [if it's possible], then we may go for it. The first quadrant of the system for all [three] variables shall be the line to cross. Do all possible case studies for the affair, involving all three parties.

Then ask over and over again, if this fact [the affair] is worth taking for the first party, for particular other, and for all others. We might need to ask, if we found a soul mate, who and whose affair could save the world. It is likely that we find a bad seed that spoils someone else, and that bad seed could spoil the whole system. Such a consequence suggests a careless judgment; we may do it because we think it is not a big deal. Once done it, it remains there forever: if it will be a mistake, it will remain as it is, even though it might be forgotten later. Unless the power of forgiveness shifts the entire coordinate plane, it will not be over.

Consider *time* would not matter here—whatever is done we would have to uphold because it must be the right choice. If we do it [tell somebody else or cross the line], we cannot turn back the course of action later. Whether the damage is enormous or minor, the fact is that we may not have time to come back to it, or that it's not worth taking that much of a risk, if our moral justification and its consequence are subject to be forgotten.

In a nutshell, the question is not 'how we learn a hard way to make judgment' It is 'what a simple way is to make justification about what we do is ethical.' Here we see it, in a few symbols. The variables and the system shown here may be applicable to many uses in our society. Each value and the relationship among each other established here hold for all kinds of facts of the variables in concern, and it is quite metaethical.

II

Design of Metaethical Organizations

Today's Planetary Influence,
Classic Tarot, Authentic I-Ching ...

Enough Reason

To <u>do</u> something ?

*From philosophical discourse
to moral counseling*

Whether It's about
Two of Coins
or Ace of Swords

*From personal dilemma
to management consulting*

... Or
It's Full Moon
or Friday Afternoon

www.metaethics.org

Introduction to Design of Metaethical Organizations
Awakening within the Old Frameworks

When you go through the recent literature in the fields of study such as organizational design, corporate structure, organizational culture, change management, strategic planning and so forth, you might have noticed that the framework and terminology used in the subjects remain by and large the same for a long time. The same concepts are being taught in classes and the same case studies are being used, as they were a decade ago, and it seems to the author that a discussion of organizational design here in this book at this point sound just dull and tedious.

It also appears that the challenges to the corporate leaders and management remain unchallenged with effective solutions by use of new frameworks and strategies, and it appears that way for a long time to come. Social sciences in these fields of study may have been out of breakthroughs in bringing new ideas, as you may notice that the students of those subjects are reading the same books as they were many years ago.

Such phenomena indicate that the basic frameworks and concepts used in the subjects of organizational behavior have been well established and as concrete and complete as they could be to this day, however decayed or unexciting they might look and sound.

The concepts introduced in the following part of this book are based on the ideas of five-dimensional analyses of causes and effects, subject matters and contexts, and the structures and conditions of our social systems. The author introduces the concept of moral autonomy and ethical succession in the fields of business ethics and management, with a hope that the attempt somehow helps revive the old subjects and stimulate interests in looking for new solutions within the wisdoms of old.

With comprehensive analyses of managerial methods and strategy planning, the author intends to provide readers with new philosophy of management and the art of designing, modeling and explaining the methods and techniques of problem solving. The interests of this book further extend to the subjects of entrepreneurship as well as the management concerns in larger organizations.

You will see basically the same diagrams that appear in this book, chapter after chapter, with different words that describe the model. The changes in the attributes of the model and the use of such changes are designed to show the fact that we can explain and analyze the situations in and out of the managerial concerns by applying the concepts of moral autonomy and the fifth dimension to the subjects in business ethics. See the logic behind the graphics of cause and effect, and consider how necessary for us, at this point, to establish new ideas and build new models of corporate design and control.

8. Metaethics in Spiral
What in Principle, How-to in Practice

Rules That Follow Practices

It is sometimes hard to find clear goals in business as people are just busy trying to get things done; it is even harder when they cannot produce wealth out of what was done. It could be the most difficult task for business people to make crystal-clear distinctions between means and goals. Even sharp people cannot make any such difference and then all gets gray and dull. Law is even murkier for the people who actually practice it. In management, like some other fields of study in business, theory often follows practice.

Giving priority to practice makes necessary that means can justify goals. Means, however, could become goals only after the previous goals were met. Making profit can be a goal but it is also a means to produce certain good, personal or common. If someone cannot feel happy about becoming rich, making money cannot be an ultimate goal, and it is not. In business ethics we can discuss someone's moneymaking practices by theorizing the behavioral patterns, but those behaviors cannot be commendable if their ends are corrupt.

Yet again, what sort of theory is that determines particular practice is morally good or not, if it follows everyday practice? Are there certain rules and regulations over every business practice? Is abiding with particular rules and regulations our ultimate goal in business? Is what is legal automatically ethical, or just morally safe if not sound? Consider your boss or fellow workers who are strict with rules, giving them credits for making efforts to help them meet their goals, and ask them what their ultimate concerns by following their rules might be. Are they actually following the rules, or following practices that have already been made their business ethics? What is their logic behind those customs?

Rules, regulations, and even theories are necessary only when our common sense fails to give us a direction to our goals. There are certain goals in management, besides just following the rules, but serving greater good in some other ways. Common sense does not make sense to us unless it works for serving common good. Rules are a set of customs or ethics, but by following such rules we can achieve only what we already planned to meet. If we found any change in our plans, we might need another set of rules that provide new prescriptions, in such a way that rules follow everyday practices. To prevent such practical means from justifying our goals, we need such a theory that makes rules.

Tragedy of an Obedient Manager

It looks awkward when someone in a managerial position firmly resists all the exceptions his or her workers requested, by simply saying, "I play by the rules." It is even sad when we see the manager getting confused and nervous about developing or adapting a new procedure, by saying, "I've never done this [operation] before," or "I'm not authorized to do this," especially if he or she is the person who likely says, "I'm the manager, ask me."

Effective managers are flexible and adaptable to changing situations by creating and changing rules, adequate in foreseeing from which direction the next wind comes, and brave when making a new move. When someone in a managerial position resists a change, small exclusion, or minor shortcut, by being strict with rules and regulations, the limits of his or her personal capacity becomes transparent. Rationales to either breaking a rule or refusing a change could be biased—there are some tricks in suggesting a change if it is by somebody of manipulative sort. Again, we need a rule for making new rules.

Managerial judgment in changing rules is often misled as unequivocal when the management tries to make a case with its moral values as the primary concern. Managerial ethics has at least two directions in practice: reasoning that preserving the rules and traditions is good, and thinking that conjuring up more spontaneity is aspiring. Besides eliminating a manager's personal motives in making judgment, the manager must make justification based on which way must be true: preserving rules to avoid mistakes or aspiring others to strive for good ends. In practice, following rules can prevent us from making wrong choices, only if those rules are intrinsically good: otherwise, why not bending and mending it?

Here in discussion, however, we are to matter those who are always strict with rules no matter what the rules are, and we try to establish the fact that legality is not always what matters most. We may say that breaking laws can be a part of traits in managerial dynamics. We may say that, if we have certain principles before those rules and regulations that strict managers cannot live without, we are morally justified when breaking rules, even if by those rules are still good enough to produce good ends. Such principles are to be found not in economics, physics or study of law, but in philosophy of ethics.

Downward Principle of Conformist Management

When someone shows cause within his or her domain of managing methods, pursuing lawful conducts makes his or her managerial capability recoil in a downward spiral. This is not a principle, but we can observe this in everyday business practices. He or she may be called control freak, and the rules and regulations in concern are the means to prevent wrong doings from becoming a managerial aim to sustain his or her cause.

Where legality matters, managerial goals are to abide employees with existing rules and regulations, so that those goals are measurable and the outcomes controllable. Those goals are planned results, the causes with a limited range of results, and the recurrences of the known facts that have already been once or more achieved.

In practice, such causes are acceptable because they are known as safe and empirically sound. However, such practices are irresolute when a change from outside brings needs for altered approaches. A management style in this practice can be frail and often perceived indecisive.

In principle, managers with predictable, internal causes have primary concerns in developing preventive measures. They are always under legitimacy pressure, for their moral principles are someone's *de facto* standards made obligatory. They use such legitimacy pressure as a fuel to accelerate their inquisitory process and strive to eliminate byproducts and spin-offs by controlling and with punishment. As the causes for fundamental changes come from the outer world of their managerial domain, there awaits the next stage of development for this management style by internal causes, beyond the realm of their managerial domain.

A simplified cause by empirical projections gives a manager less courage to face unknown reality, and the leader's capability narrows down. The manager cannot outgrow his or her autonomous domain as his or her controllability may increase within the domain. Such a phenomenon is observed in rule-centered management practices and perceived as downward [or inward], the principle that becoming overly concerned with internal causes impedes the manager's advancement in his or her own development. In principle, such management style imposes moral obligation; in practice, the worst outcomes take the form of ethical regression.

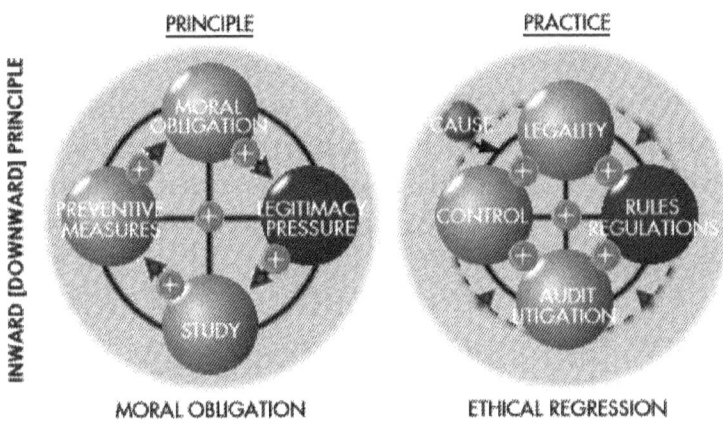

Figure 8. Inward Principle and Ethical Regression

Upward Principle of Spontaneous Management

Another style of management to be considered is that focuses on striving for guidance and aspiring others, rather than giving them a burden of obedience. The basis of the management action in this style is the ability to strive for guidance even for causes that are unfamiliar or unknown.

Taken outside cause that is unknown, reliance on our own developed consciousness and common sense, both in principle and in practice, can either put us on the right track or leave us astray. The ability to cope with uncertainty of such outer causes derives from the increased knowledge and skills in deciding-making. The effective means to provide others with right solutions in unfamiliar situations is the leader's expanded capacity for tolerance toward uncertainty, and the leader's domain of moral autonomy must develop to make the uncertain, certain. Such development of a leader's autonomy requires his or her continuing study in the knowledge of ethical behavior, so that the leader becomes capable of building new logistics for managing changes in an organization.

In practice, the management may have less applicable laws to either explain or solve the situation that may occur, and hence a manager needs to rely on his or her common sense to begin with the challenge at the time of turmoil. Since the outcome of the management action is not yet known, nor predictable, the situation presents an opportunity for the manager to exercise the most creative and constructive forms and measures of leadership.

In principle, this type of increased consciousness and resulting managerial actions would inspire people, and can be used as a tool of enlightenment as well as empowerment. The goal of the management is moral aspiration, and the growth stage of this type of management is in a state of ethical succession.

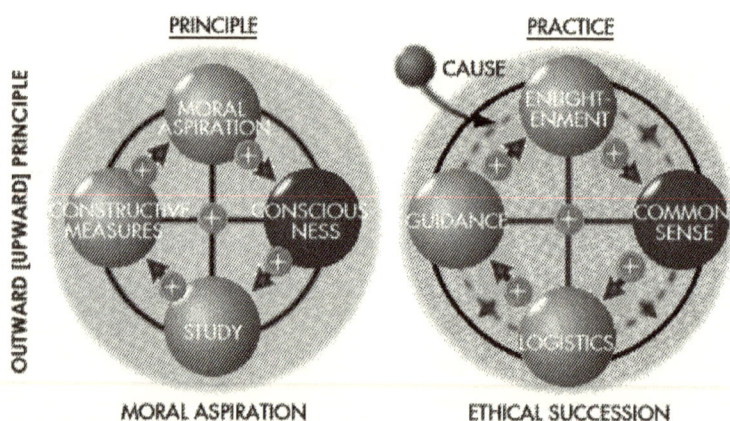

Figure 9. Outward Principle and Ethical Succession

9. Spontaneous Management as a System
True State of Spontaneity in Management

Understanding the upward principle of spontaneous management, one's spontaneity is understood as a management style as well as the way to his or her ethical succession. Now, in order to experience this spontaneous style of management in a business, managers need to be aware of its own risk: *Does spontaneity go well with systematizing?*

As long as doing business as a sole proprietor without employees, virtually taking care of everything by themselves, managers may not worry too much about their own working styles. Expanding a business, however, requires much more attention to developing a system, in which someone else can take over the owner's roles when necessary.

In this short course of analysis, let us take a closer look at how spontaneity can be exercised in a larger business system. The following hypotheses need to be proven as a fact that weighs much of a thought on the true state of spontaneity.

Hypothesis 1
H0: If it is just a style, spontaneity in managerial layers would not work in a system.
H1: Spontaneity holds validity as a style of ideal management system in a multi-headed business entity.

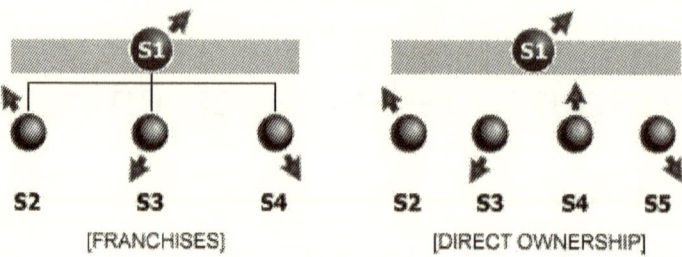

Figure 10. Spontaneity Layers in Franchises and Direct Ownership

Depending on its nature of business, the owner of a business has a choice of legal form in expanding a business, whether franchising or branching out under direct ownership. Take the spontaneity exercised by both franchisees and branch managers as a variable that affects business performances of the entire company.

Since it is just a variable management style, subordinates' spontaneity may or may not agree with the owner's own way of doing. It could be chaotic if all top management head toward different directions, bringing in their own style and agenda in the first place.

Hypothesis 2

H0: Spontaneity needs to be understood by subordinates but need not be exercised by all others.

H1: Managers need to brainwash subordinates in order to practice their own spontaneity through others.

The objective of a spontaneous manager in this case is very simple: *Make sure that every other knows what a lesson is when leading by example in a spontaneous way.* Some of the subordinates may respond: wherever you go, we go. Others might argue: whatever you do, you do anyway. Isn't it just enough to exercise one's spontaneity, whichever his or her subordinate might say? Or does a manager need his or her personal style and make others follow that example?

This is the style of conformist management, which leads to ethical regression, even if the manager's style can be systematized to some degrees. Enforcing a style relies solely on the legitimacy of the one who started his or her own way. A business conducted in this way may live one lifetime, or just one term, but its growth may be limited.

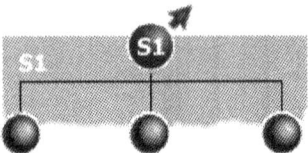

Figure 11. Understood but not Enforced Spontaneity

Hypothesis 3

H0: Somebody needs to take over or inherit spontaneity so that it becomes systematized.

H1: Managers need to brainwash subordinates in order to practice their own spontaneity through others.

This is a tricky situation: the owner may have to find and discipline particular someone who can understand the owner's way, exercise his or her way, and enforce it to others. Does the owner need to brainwash him or her? If the owner's right-hand person is smart enough to be the owner's own counselor or a mentor, this style might work well.

The question is: *Is the owner smart enough to know where he or she is leading?* Since the owner's spontaneity is understood as the company's inner cause of obedience, this may hold up exercises of innovative ideas and decisive actions at a time of change.

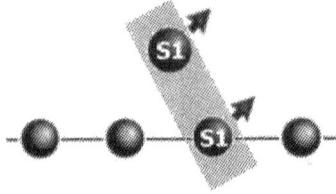

Figure 12. Systematized Spontaneity with Inner Causes

Hypothesis 4

H0: Spontaneity as a system requires external causes to be systematized.

H1: Spontaneity loses its own reason to exist if it is guided by external causes.

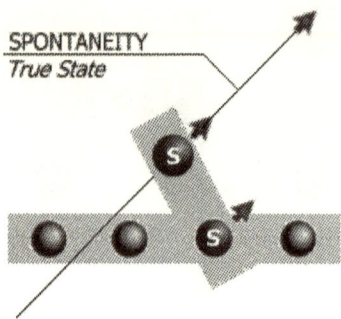

Figure 13. Spontaneity as a System—True State of Spontaneity

Spontaneity is not only the means to get a job done but also an instrument of empowering the whole system in which a business operates. Empowerment does not occur unless the entire system experiences a fundamental change at every level, and to experience such a state, spontaneity is required at all levels.

The true state of spontaneity is more than somebody's management style if the purpose of a management practice is to manage a change brought by an external cause. This state concerns the top management's autonomy that absorbs spontaneity at all levels of a company. A direction of change is set by something other than what the company has experienced, and everyone's spontaneity must be set towards such a direction. It is not the owner's own version of spontaneity in practice that needs to be understood, but it is the ability to be spontaneous when needed that needs to be incorporated as a system.

Proven all the above hypotheses, a manager should know that his or her spontaneity is not just for finding opportunities for his or her own use. True state of spontaneity requires a manager to see if his or her spontaneity is directed towards the expansion of autonomy for the entire company. One person could do this all the time in a business where nobody else is working for him or her, and that would be exercised as one's ethical succession. In larger organizations, the true state of spontaneity functions as the entire company's succession, and spontaneity becomes the agent of a fundamental change.

10. Perplexity of Managerial Knowledge
In the Cases of Sales and Marketing Management

While *marketing* practices involve broader range of activities and processes, *sales* can be understood and then practiced as an essential part of such a marketing activity or process. Marketing is the activity or process involving research, promotion, sales, and distribution of a product or service. Compared to sales practices, marketing includes not only sales, but also the activities and other parts of a whole process before and after sales activities occur. Sales managers concentrate on strict elements of their positions in conducting sales, rather than managing overall process of marketing activities.

Sales Management

Definitions of Sales

Sales are an activity or case of selling goods or services. The art of sales, or what is called *salesmanship* means the skills and techniques used in selling goods or services. Sales practices are based mostly on the science of human behavior, as well as experience and making judgment. Sales practice, therefore, is practically a name of the game ruled by the law of perception, which entails the truth considered highly relative to people's mind. Therefore, the skills and techniques used in sales activities are specific. Salespeople must identify the critical issues facing the buyer, by listening actively to their customers and prospects. Then they need to apply their outputs, products and/or services, to their buyers' perception in order to meet their demand.

Definitions of Sales Management

Sales managers need to provide knowledge and experience in determining the right product mix, the right promotional methods, and the right locations that could be conceived as space-time, in order to enhance the productivity of sales practices. Sales management is a concept of managing activities of salespeople. Its management practices have a functional focus on activities, rather than the wide range of an entire marketing process. Its effectiveness is centered in providing the knowledge needed to support sales operations. Its efficiency is measured by such control variables, as contribution to profit, return on assets, sales cost ratio, market share, and achievement of other tangible goals. Implementation of sales management may take a longer period, and hence is a part of a long-term training and development process. However, such a program must be understood as the one that involves the resources primarily engaged in sales activities but less in other activities of a business or company.

How Sales Differs from Marketing

The effectiveness of practices in getting results through sales is essential to the overall marketing effort and significantly affects a company's profit and loss. While marketing practices involve broader range of activities and processes, sales can be understood and practiced as an essential part of such a marketing activity or process. Sales tactics mostly include the skills and techniques used in the act of selling itself, rather than designing, manufacturing and distributing a product or service, or forecasting and determining what and how much the market demand is.

Marketing Management

Definitions of Marketing

Marketing is an activity or process involving research, promotion, sales, and distribution of a product or service. Tactics may differ in small sized businesses from that used in larger businesses. For small businesses in particular, marketing investment is primarily the time and energy of entrepreneurs and those who support their leaders, as well as their own power of imagination. In traditional marketing that concerns larger corporations, marketing requires investment in building its process, the system that would work for all the activities from production to sales.

Definitions of Marketing Management

It may be acceptable to say that marketing practices include everything to do to promote a business on regular basis. Since marketing is a process, its managerial process is a course of determining the requirements of a market, *e.g.*, customer's wants, needs, and demands, and a course of satisfying that demand through manufacturing, distribution, pricing, promotion, after-sales services, and financing for the entire process. Marketing managers may engage not only in developing and controlling the activities of salespeople. They may also undertake formulating and implementing the strategies for designing and packaging a brand or product, and engage in projecting the demand of both the entire market and specific group of customers. Marketing management includes the role of sales management and the role of overseeing the entire marketing process, and therefore, it must be the exercise of wider capacity and hence it is to maintain well-built connections with both production side and finance division of a corporation.

How Marketing Differs from Sales

Compared to sales practices, marketing includes not only sales, but also research and development that are the activities and part of a process before promotion and sales occur. Marketing also includes distribution that covers before (from suppliers to manufacturing) and after (from production to end users) the periods of sales activities. Therefore, marketing managers would assume more responsibilities in a business than sales managers. If appointed separately, marketing managers may take general and accommodating responsibilities to support sales managers who would focus on the activities of salespeople.

Design and Function of Management Process

Whether marketing managers should supervise sales managers, or they both work together as peers, depends on which design is more efficient and effective in an organization. It must be noted, however, that we must not confuse marketing effectiveness with sales effectiveness. The knowledge used in the activities and its operational efficiency are more focused and specific in sales operations and much broader in marketing. Sales managers concentrate on specified elements of their positions in conducting sales, rather than managing overall process of marketing activities.

Notice the differences in management power and authority to be exercised in sales management and marketing management. A manager's autonomous domain is larger in marketing than in sales, and so wider the range of responsibilities in marketing. The location of knowledge determines what type of decision-making must take place, and a department's operational effectiveness and efficiency need to be measured by different control variables. It is a management question to define what decisions to make, and each department is responsible for making specific decision. By understanding such authenticity of knowledge and the definition of operational responsibilities the management can specify the difference between sales and marketing.

Consider also, however, a concept of moral autonomy or spontaneous management can be equally applied to both sales and marketing management practices. Perplexity of managerial knowledge originates in a confused state that different principles must apply to different kinds of practices; such thinking may result in setting different rules for moral justification used in different departments of an organization. Organizational design requires common sets of rules, and that rules must not follow the nature of practices; instead practices need to adopt commonly accepted principles. Such principles can be understood in metaethical definitions of what kind of principle is required to direct the entire organization into one direction.

Management processes and activities of either sales or marketing can be divided into two categories—subject matters handled in a department and different types of labor to be used (division of labor). Responsibilities of the management in either department are measurable in the same manners when the same principle is to be applied to make the rules for justifying the management behavior. The difference in managerial knowledge is based solely on the scale of autonomy of the management, not on specific practices or skills in the first place. Managerial knowledge acquired in this way produces an effective general manager, whose knowledge in decision-making is valid and sound regardless of the unit to manage, and such knowledge is definitive and can be applied to making judgment in any other parts of an organization.

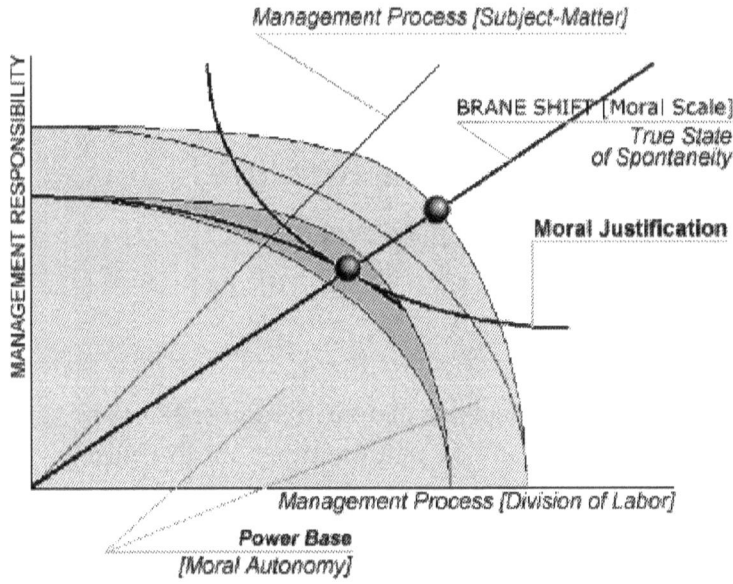

Figure 14. Design and Function of Management Process in Metaethics

11. Philosophy of Risk Assessment
Dimensions of Project Risk and Management Procedures

Risk assessment of a project must come in numbers—not necessarily to rely on the statistics at any cost all the time, but to realize how much future liability could be and what to do in case, as liability is to eventually counterbalance one's asset. We cannot always rely on numbers as the outcomes of a probability table, but project risks need to be quantified one way or the other. Such numbers help the management realize the need to exposure and admit the existence of potential liabilities and disclose the associated risks. Liability thus quantified does exist in any business and constitutes the right-hand side of a balance sheet.

Risk assessment in project management is, therefore, to come up with the numbers that would tell the management what and how much the possibility of hazard, danger, or damage might be, in terms of financial loss. Risk assessment is also a procedure to expose the management to the potential loss in and out of a project and have them recognize such a chance of exposé.

Although risk assessment procedures and tools are subject to change, there are commonly acceptable definitions of terms and basic rules, steps and systems to identify and quantify the risks of a project. Here are those basics to be understood and the systems for project managers to use as well as to renew, revise and re-develop procedures and practices.

Definitions of Project

Projects discussed in project management are not only of tangible or technical matters, such as programs, systems, products and services. Projects can be any extensive undertaking of mindful, deliberate, professional, or academic concerns. Project can be performed as a single task, or can be a set of joint or diversified acts and responsibilities.

Project category varies from a simple and routine job at a store or a task in an office, to a complex and often labor-intensive effort in a larger scale, artistic or creative pursuit of body and mind. The definition of project would further extend its reach, from somebody's hobby or recreation, to maneuvers concerning personal, group or national efforts, or even to one's spiritual quest for the meaning of life.

A project gives such a cause that falls on a surface or an exterior of an event that someone observes and evaluates it. It is a quality external to and independent of conscious vocation, in either individual or collective sense. Local, distant, hedging or strictly positioned, a project is a focal act of alerted individuals, to externally focus their attentions, consciousness and their professions upon a surface of something, somebody or a group that would benefit from the probable outcomes. Subjective, objective or inter-subjective, it is to draw a projection of conceptualization to a form of creation or artifact.

A project in project management, therefore, needs to be evaluated in the terms that the observers and the addressees of the project can comprehend. The use of numerical terms would assist those who evaluate a project with better ideas of the outcomes. Those numbers would also help those who carry a project better realize the likelihood of results in quantitative values, when they are exposed to the risks associated with the project, the risk of not accomplishing the planed consequences.

Elements of Risk

A project risk is a possibility of damage or loss incurred because of the failures to accurately draw a picture of certain projection of concentrated work as particular product and manifestation of a concept. For project managers, a failure of a project is scaled as the cost of producing defects or flaws, in which the possible risk factors should be identified.

Usually the risks of a project include the following failures to overcome. Those are:

- The failure to obtain all the anticipated benefits—financial or qualitative
- The failure to prevent cost overrun of implementation
- The failure to prevent time shortage, and as a result, elapsed time for implementation
- The failure to prevent technical shortfall or defect in resulting outputs, products, systems or services
- The failure to prevent incompatibility, noncompliance or inappropriateness of the outcomes
- The failure to prevent resource imbalance, such as that in staffing and material uses, due to abuse, misuse and mismanagement.

In addition to the risk elements of a single job, the overall risk factors of combined tasks may also need to be identified and assessed. Those risk elements include:

- The failure to assess individual project risk and to consider the aggregate risk of the portfolio of tasks
- The lack of recognition that different projects may require different project structures, planning and analytical tools, managerial approaches, integration methods and control mechanisms.

Risk Identification and Feasibility Study

Based on the list of risk elements, a project manager needs to figure out in what categories or dimensions to identify the risks of particular project. There are several dimensions or perspectives to find the risks, such as:

- Size and nature of the project, in monetary expenses, estimated completion time, staffing levels, skill inputs, and the number and functions of groups to be affected
- Likelihood of technology substitution, trend shift, or any other changes that would require certain skill levels and knowledge areas to be thoroughly covered, in order to anticipate alterations in plans and outcomes
- Management and project structures that define the outcomes, from the vary start of the project, based on the notion that the quality of inputs determines the resulting quality. The quality of products may be highly affected by the knowledge of what the outputs would or should be, and the consensus levels to be reached beforehand.
- In addition to the technical considerations in areas, depth and time, the potential change or loss in moral values may also need to be considered as the risks in numerical terms. If the results of a project would jeopardize the survival or the good reasons for future existence of the individual or parts of an organization, such concerns should be addressed. Abuse or misuse of power, authority, or discretion granted to a task force may damage the moral values of those who are in the operation, and that must be a management concern.

Risk Assessment

Practically addressed, risk assessment in project management is conducted in the form of a spreadsheet analysis. A risk assessment worksheet would list all the identified risks classified by the risk category, each of which would carry a different degree of risk to be scaled and quantified.

Each one of the individual risk factors needs to be rated and may be weighted by distinguishing the relative scale of its own risk. Then, the aggregate risk score, or the overall risk, of all risk factors combined or all individual tasks or projects combined as a portfolio, must be measured.

It may be useful to construct reference charts or diagrams for the assessed risk levels, in order to estimate the contingency or liability in quantifiable values by linking those risk levels to monetary values. This practice is also applicable to determining the original and additional costs of the projects and/or the price of the outputs. The information is further useful for assigning the approval level for the projects, especially in larger corporations with more layers and divisions of management level.

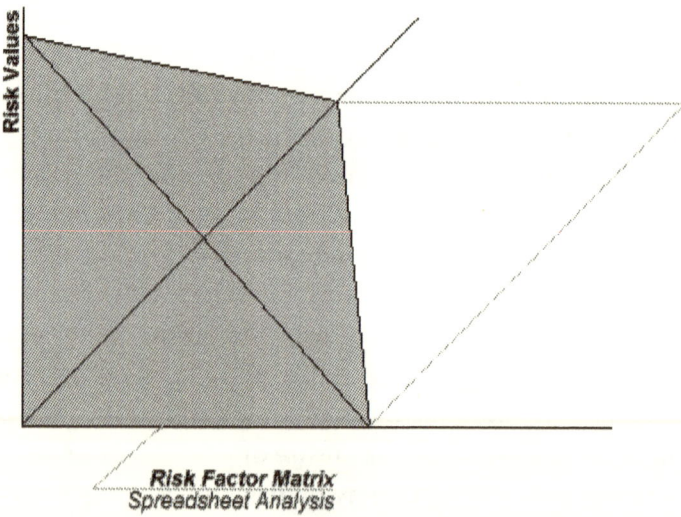

Figure 15. Reference Diagrams for Risk Assessment

Approval as External Causes

At this stage of approving a project, a decisive approach is required to ensure that adequate cost-benefit analyses be conducted. In this approach, it is crucial to consider how the benefits would offset the risks, by evaluating tangible benefit, gross profit and net income as the result of a project.

In some organizations, it may also include estimating apportioned budget and resources for the individuals or divisions responsible for the project, and permissions in liquidating other sources of budget or income due to any failure or loss that incurred in the project. It is also important to discuss how much, in monetary values, a person, a company or a division can recover from the loss by implementing or instigating relatively more profitable or financially substantial projects and dealings. For projects of higher risks, in both a large organization with a complex structure and a small business with limited resources, the consideration of such recovery plans may be essential from financial viewpoints.

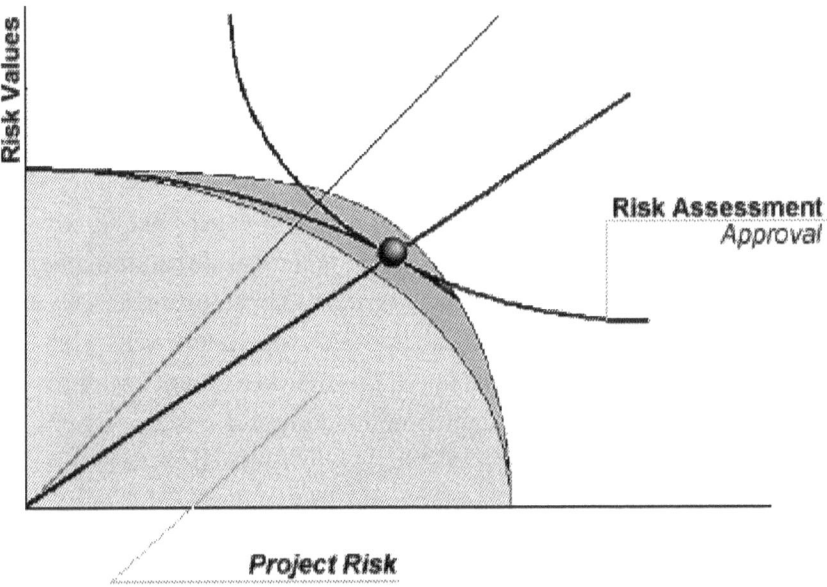

Figure 16. Project Approval as External Causes

Appropriate Risk Assessment and Project Management Structure

In organizational design and for technological compliance, it is a mandate to establish appropriate structures for both risk assessment and project management. Any decision criteria used by assessment professionals can be subjective, and any future technological progress on which knowledge and tools are to be based may be uncertain. It may be difficult to find some universally applicable rules to evaluate risks, nor to obtain such multi-purpose methods to manage and control many projects of different kinds. However, implementing successful projects requires development of reliable assessment structure, planning tools, systems integration methods and control mechanisms.

Formation of such structures and devices are also part of evaluation criteria in the risk assessment phase of a project.

- Assessment Structure

  Risk assessment needs to be conducted by the experts, internal or external, with sufficient skills, knowledge and experience in concern. Such faculties or groups may include technical, legal, and financial staffs, as well as counselors and mentors. Those professionals using distinct criteria should assess each project, together or separately, and then a project manager needs to obtain their agreement or approval to proceed. They may periodically hold meetings for risk assessment, status review and action plans in a critical project. These functions and events for assessment can be made into a procedure.

- Planning Tools

  The professionals from various areas of science have developed formal planning tools for various projects. Project managers should apply some of the commonly used planning tools, such as PERT [P(rogram) E(valuation and) R(eview) T(echnique)], critical path, networking methods and other diagrams for locating data and knowledge, and make sure that those plans thus obtained be followed when implementing a project.

- Integration Methods
  Depending on the nature of a project, those effective means of processes, technology, or systems integration may include either internal or external groups of professionals, technicians, managers, users, observers alike. Project leaders and teams must have discussions on technical and managerial issues among those participants to increase efficiency, effectiveness, accuracy, control, compatibility, and compliance level of the project and its outcomes.

- Control Mechanisms
  In critical projects, contingency plans must be discussed regularly in a meeting involving those risk assessment experts and other aides, initiated by the project manager, sales department or marketing sector in charge of a project. A decision process may involve supervisors or higher management for alternative, hedge plans or diversifications for the coverage of future risks and actual deviations from the original plans.

After taken all the above steps and considerations, however, there still might be other contingencies and uncertainties to a project. These methods and procedures do not describe all the possible losses and liabilities. They would only work to give an estimate of a plan for preventing a huge or total loss at once.

Such risk assessment processes are as a preventive mechanism that would give project managers some assured thoughts that liability exist for sure. Then the management can minimize the damage by reducing the risk areas, levels and dimensions by planning and taking appropriate preventive actions. None of projects can be risk-free, as any business has its own liability concerns.

Risk assessment is a management tool for exposure, admission and disclosure of chances and responsibilities as risks. Since it is an instrument that may expire, a risk assessment itself needs to be diagnosed, monitored, and re-tooled, as long as a liability exists. The inclination or temptation of the management to undermine, ignore and screen risks may persist or recur.

A good reason for enduring with effective assessment tools, which helps create hope in a project, must follow the philosophy of a leader who is capable of making decisions acceptable to wider audience of a project. The risks of a project immediately represent the autonomy of someone who leads the project. A manager's capability is measured by the power and authority that gains the approval of a project by the assessment body that exists as an external cause to the project.

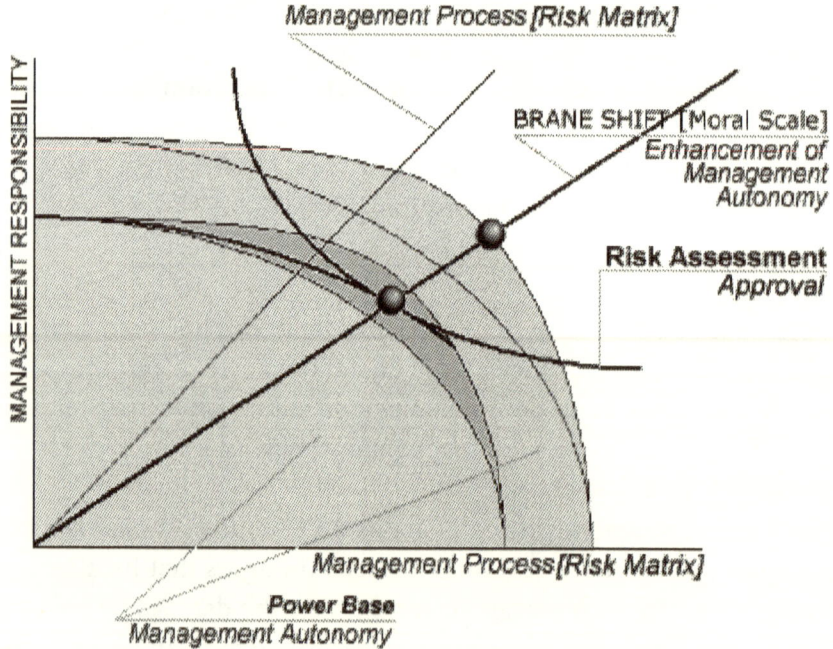

Figure 17. Management Capability in Risk Assessment

12. Managerial Issues in Building Matrix Structures of Organizations
Supplement to Philosophy of Risk Assessment

Matrix Management: Functions and Benefits

Matrix management was in fashion in the past, but it has sunk in many rigid organizational structures over time and failed to perform its original purposes of keeping a company agile and coordinating activities across divisions. Later, matrix structures were renewed in the form of empowered business teams, as well as a token for virtual organizations and rightsizing. Generally, product development and customer satisfaction are better served with matrix arrangements, with a focus around business processes that cut horizontally across divisions.

In economics as well as in mathematics, matrix is a rectangular array of elements displayed as rows and columns. All elements are the array themselves, and members of the field are set out in rows and columns. Matrices may be of any dimension, with any number of rows and columns, meaning that in a corporation a line manager can invite participations in decision-making from different functional managers, and vice versa. Matrix is used to facilitate the solution of problems such as the transformation of coordinates, which in business means the corporate transformation of values and decision-making processes.

First and the foremost important part of understanding a matrix structure in management is that the product of matrices is defined only if they
are conformable. Two managers in row and column cannot perform a
joint decision-making without being confocal, having a common focus, in
the operation of the field in which they are located. Another important
factor in designing a matrix management is that, as conventional wisdom
in mathematics dictates, in all dealings with matrices the row is designated
first. This means that somebody has to have a primary responsibility in a
business operation, and that has to be of a line manager. If the responsibilities of a line manager and a functional manager are obscured by the conflicts of interests between them, the line manager needs to take an
initiative. In other words, the power edge belongs to the line leader, who is
a generalist and set out in a row of a matrix, and functions serve the line by
nurturing specialists and advancing their state of the art performances.

Many of sustainable approaches to strategic thinking in organizations in the past have focused the attention of managers on building
competence and capabilities in a set of corporate resources. Matrix
management has been an approach to a resource-based strategy in
practice, which was used to make a company's resources drive its performance in a dynamic competitive environment as a new framework
that moves strategic thinking forward. The research results by many
corporations indicate that matrices still are the dominant approach for
completing development projects. However, adopting intricate organizational matrices has in some cases shortcomings due to its functional-
ity; the matrix design is particularly vulnerable to the conflicts of
interests between managers and among the teams they form. It is a mis-
taken belief that matrix management is the same as group decision-
making; its power relation between the row and column of the matrix
reveals both success and failure factors of a matrix design. The key issue
is the failure to recognize different types of matrices: there are three
matrix structures, *pure* (functional), *balanced*, and *project* matrices.

In a basic scheme of matrix management, two managers, one a line manager whose responsibilities are set in a row, and the other across-the-board, functional manager whose responsibilities are set in a column, are to share the resources and cooperate for a development task in which they are engaged. In a pure or functional matrix, two managers are considered equal in exercising decision-making or influence power. In a balanced matrix, the responsibilities and decisions thus made can be balanced by weighing the capabilities and expertise of two managers in concern. In either case, both line manager and functional manager are at equal position.

That immediately presents a problem of ambiguity of reporting to two bosses, because two managers have the same job responsibilities. In the matrix structure from the concept of a pure or balanced matrix, two bosses were equal, meaning that real power was up for grabs between two bosses, and thus has resulted in conflict and delay in reaching a decision. In many actual cases, these matrix forms were simply pasted over the already rigid hierarchy in place, without pondering those possible conflicts.

Mostly adopting project matrices can attain the actual improvement in job performance. While all three types of matrices have comparable usage rates, the project matrix is considered the most effective one. Suppose two managers participate in a development project. A line manager has its own division of marketing forces, while the other, called project manager, responds only to a specific project among many job accounts that the line management holds. In a sales department, a line manager may have many customers, and a project manager may either take care of one customer or a specific project of that customer, depending on the certified skill areas and interests of the project manager. In a product development line, a line manager may have many products, and a project manager may handle the development of specific product or feature. The project manager may have his or her own resources chosen for a development of products, while the line manager and his or her human resources may team up with the project manager to represent the entire case. Financial responsibilities can be shared or separated between two sections. For example, the project manager can pay for extra materials or services needed for a development task, while some other expenses used by both a sales person from the line manager's office and an engineer from the project management team in one occasion can be divided into two accounts. Each member of the entire task can choose a report line between the line manager and the project manager, depending on the nature of the decision to be made.

Keeping a company strategically flexible and adaptable while coordinating its activities across divisions requires eliminating narrow scope of partisanship and improving open communication. The goal is to build a matrix of priorities in decision-making in the frame of minds of managers, from both row and column of the field.

Logic behind Matrix Design of Organizations

It is important to notice that the purpose and practice of building a matrix structure in an organization do not end in formatting a spreadsheet. Design of matrix structure is neither a responsibility of a line manager or a project manager, but that of a company executive who oversees the entire operation. Finding a compatible and conformable mix of lines and projects is the only beginning of the design. Next the management needs to allocate resources and measure overall job and sales performance of the company, and that measure must be set as an independent scale to the matrix design. The performance level of a matrix design forms a three-dimensional design of an organization, and the area or volume obtained as a result of such operation represents the company's effectiveness, by and large.

Increasing the effectiveness of particular organization design reflects the top management's responsibilities, and that in turn represents the adequacy and sufficiency of the management. The logic behind the matrix design of an organization is found in such a multi-dimensional analysis of the company's effectiveness.

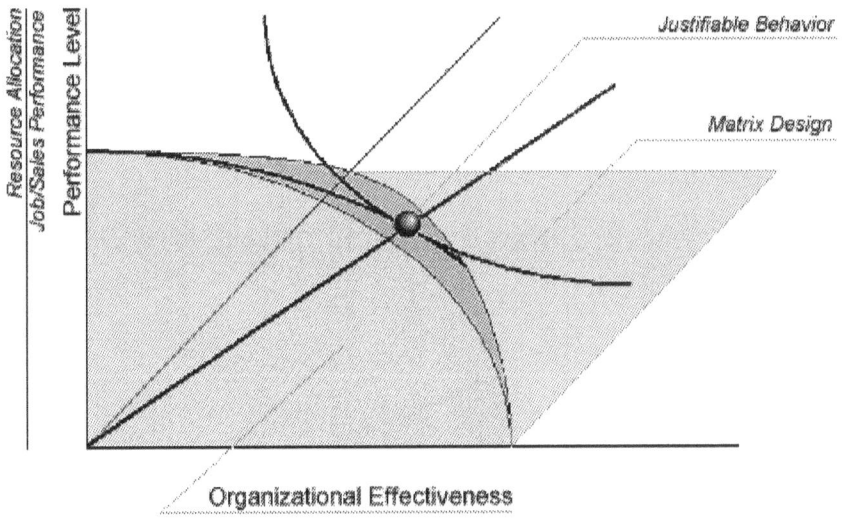

Figure 18. Multi-Dimensional Framework of Organizational Design

Since we already discussed the power base and the use of authority by the management in a five-dimensional framework earlier in this book, it may not be necessary to repeat the concept of autonomy and its structure in this chapter to avoid redundancy. The point to be made, however, is that a company's effectiveness cannot be evaluated in some simple two-dimensional models of cost and benefit, risk and return, supply and demand, or such a kind of trade-offs. The causes and effects of an organizational effectiveness need to be understood with a concept of what is affected by the company's performance and who evaluates, accepts and approves, such a performance.

Justification of a company's performance is given by the outer sources of the company, and responsibilities of the management need to absorb and address the functions and criteria of the audience who observe the company's performance. Needless to say, the autonomy of the management must be wide and large in scope and size, and consistent and reliable in its quality, enough for the audience to use the understanding and awareness of the management as the facts to base their judgment for or against the company's behavior.

13. Empowerment: By Design or Default?

Philosophy of Designing Empowerment Programs in Organizations

Empowerment by Design and by Default

When organizational design is much talked about, many analysts would agree that the change strategies must involve encouraging participation from the organization's constituencies. Fundamental changes in the business environment require finding the solutions to enhanced organizational capability, which is the product of the organization's adaptive culture to change. A design for organizational change in structure must entail, or must be followed by, re-constructed social norms that work as the default, collective culture that absorbs such a change. In employee empowerment, a design needs to be made to re-condition default customs, in which way structures would sustain ideal forms of organizations.

In social science, a discussion of empowerment is not about whether a structure must follow a form, or vice versa. Ideal forms of knowledge are far beyond the boundary that any studies in social science can reach. Grand design is set forth to create default in the first place, while default accommodates all available options to design, and there would be no contradictions between their origins. Such argument is metaphysically correct when it comes to the ultimate human understanding of things in general. In organizational design and employee empowerment, it is the balance and the set of priorities between default and design that needs to be addressed. In addition, it is a management agenda and responsibility to ensure that such organizational actions of empowerment necessitate both external (structural) compliance and internal (motivational) commitment, side by side.

By design, empowerment must be incorporated within the structure and system, which bind a company's business conducts. Here, we argue report structure, job design, procedures and code of conducts; we discuss not instantly deductive methods from a concept of grand design but the conclusion from observation and experience of regularity and integration. The default set of corporate values and behaviors are reliable information and visible among the employees who accept and participate in their company's culture. By default, empowerment must be integrated as a set of pre-determined options adopted when no alternative norms or schemes are specified. The culture of an organization itself must allow the models and re-models of empowerment schemes to exist and engage in its default culture.

In order for managers to protect their companies from control failures when employees are empowered, managers need to allow employees to initiate process improvements in effective manners. When the tools to reconcile the conflict between initiative and control are at hand, employee empowerment by design can co-exist with the empowerment originated within the company by default. Belief systems that communicate core values and inspire all the participants to commit to the organization's purpose would form the environment, and its organizational culture, that can work as the platform for employee empowerment. On the other hand, the company's structures and systems establish borderline rules and identify consequences and drawbacks, and hence they function as a planned, designed scheme of empowerment. Control mechanism can be built within both formats, culture by default and structure by design, to allow higher management to diagnose and ensure efficiency and effectiveness of those instruments.

Bad examples for such culture and system, of course, can be observed everywhere in our business environment, such as grapevine among peers and tiers, bickering between strata, poor union relations, nit-picking work rules, unnecessary layers and report lines, and so on. Empowerment is a much talked about subject in management; but it may not seem working in many organizations where top management carefully undermine it, middle managers faintly downplay it, and workers subtly demoralize any new responsibilities that empowerment may entail.

Empowerment may entail two kinds of commitment, external and internal. First, external commitment is a contractual compliance under a command-and-control model. This is the product of a structure-oriented approach to empowerment: the system that follows organizational design. Any report structures, reward programs, and code of conducts that help the management empower their workers, may fall into this category. Second, internal commitment is a self-disciplinary fulfillment that occurs for the workers' own individual reasons and motives. Hence, internal commitment is much more directly related to empowerment. The problem with any organizational change programs designed to encourage empowerment is that they actually end up creating more external than internal commitment. Change management must avoid that the design requires extra modifications and re-designs in the company's exteriors; it must pursue that new visions and values are absorbed in the company's culture and are engaged with the workers, ultimately, by default.

Empowerment of First Line Managers: What Goes Wrong?

When it comes to the empowerment of lower line managers, there needs to be mentioned another common failure of motivational schemes that covers up many functional and psychological problems that the empowerment is supposed to overcome. It is the failure of localizing the knowledge—information and acquaintance—of authority and responsibility to be transferred or delegated.

In order to fight poor motivation and lack of commitment, business owners and higher managers have a challenge in changing their management style and redesigning the structure of the company. By giving up their own authority and getting employees in lower tiers to take full responsibility for whatever decisions made in conditions of business conduct and performance, higher management can ensure contractual designs for employee empowerment. Few entrepreneurs, however, easily give up their authority and responsibility. In larger organizations, there can be found procedural difficulties and emotional distresses of middle managers, who have their boss's responsibility without the boss's authority. The reason for such dilemmas is that top managers are inclined to securing their benefits derived from their hard-earned authority. By design, delegation of authority must take place in an organization, segment by segment. However, it is far more important that the responsibilities can be shared as common values, by default, whereas the authority of each segment can vary by context and condition.

Many businesses over time approach a turning point in organizational structure, lines of authority, and job designs and responsibility. Delegation of authority by design needs to be understood by how formal the delegated authority is, in accordance to the extent of its authenticity; delegation needs to be performed in accordance with what content and context it must be transferred. Both of these considerations would help managers realize clarified responsibilities for their representation and exercise of their granted knowledge and power.

Such a scheme or design of authority transfer, and thus empowerment of lower line managers, need to be grounded to the knowledge and experience of clear distinction between authority and responsibility. Such distinction may be formalized by codes and designs of new corporate and job structure. However, such a feature of organizational design needs to be rooted deeply into the organizational cultures and values, which in turn manifest in the company's norms and common practice by default. For those who assimilate authorities and exercise responsibilities, it is the knowledge of authority and responsibility that will justify power allocations, moralize empowerment, and direct one's internal commitment to performance and effectiveness.

14. On Change Management
The Logic of the Models of Change Management

Change in business involves factors that themselves change over time and over the social and economic conditions of the environment. The models of change management to be discussed, of course, constantly need to be created, modified, and adapted as the economic and techno-logical environment change. The ways of thinking and the models set forth in the past may or may not work in the new era of marketing and technology in the future. The forms of discussion need to be dealt with a caution to the applicability of the models to describe the contents of and the solutions to fundamental change in businesses. The basic logic applied here, is that a change in businesses contains at least two major sets of factors: that of economic (or environmental) factors and that of organizational (or cultural) factors. Finding a perfect match and the balance between those two sets of change factors shall be the main agenda of change management, and hence the ideal roles of leadership must be to describe and prescribe both structural and cultural aspects of change in an organization.

On Definition of Fundamental Change in Business

Managing change in businesses has been an either/or proposition: either quickly to create economic value for shareholders or patiently develop an open, trusting corporate culture in a long run. Combining such economic approaches and organizational, cultural approaches can radically transform the way businesses change.

Change Models

Economic modeling of change usually involves heavy use of financial incentives, drastic layoffs, downsizing and restructuring. In such modeling procedures, shareholder value is usually considered the most important and legitimate measure of corporate success. This approach is about maximizing shareholder value as a goal, and the leadership style involved herein is *top down*, with an emphasis on rebuilding structure and systems. The adapted mechanism involves financial incentives as the most commonly applicable measurement for motivation.

On the other hand, considering organizational change models is used toward building up a new set of corporate culture that concerns employee behaviors, attitudes, capabilities, and commitment. In such an approach, the organization's ability to learn from its experiences is considered a legitimate yardstick of corporate success. This approach has a primary focus on developing organizational capabilities, as the output of collective organizational culture, which is the totality of employee behaviors and attitudes. The change strategies involve encouraging participation from the organization's constituencies, and hence the leadership style here adapted is *bottom up*. This approach takes commitment from the company's employees as a promise that ensures the rewards and motivation among those who participate in a change process.

Change Management

Managing change is considered the art of balancing the content of change and the participants' acts. The vehicle for the change in businesses shall be made up of such a balanced approach in leadership, in order for the management to increase certainty in a system and capability among those who are in the system.

To secure flexibility in a new economy structure, companies must build up their adaptive corporate cultures and increase shareholder value. There must be a balance and match between the theory of economic modeling and theory of organizational modeling in change management. A balanced approach in simultaneously setting goals on both structures and instruments of an organization can be used effectively for spontaneous change in the environment and the organization's plans, processes and procedures.

On Leadership in Change Management

The complexity of conformity to a change in an organization and its environment may not be as easy to be handled as solving technical problems. The challenge to leadership in change management is to find solutions to building a flexible structure and adaptive culture in the collective intelligence of its employees.

Roles of Leadership in Change Management

To successfully manage transitions in a business and its environment, the leaders initiating or navigating through a change need a fair approach in re-modeling a corporate structure and building a new corporate culture. Such an approach includes several steps—to define the subjects of change, to establish the contexts for change, to provide resources in order to stimulate involvement, and to coordinate convergent values, attitudes and behaviors among the participants.

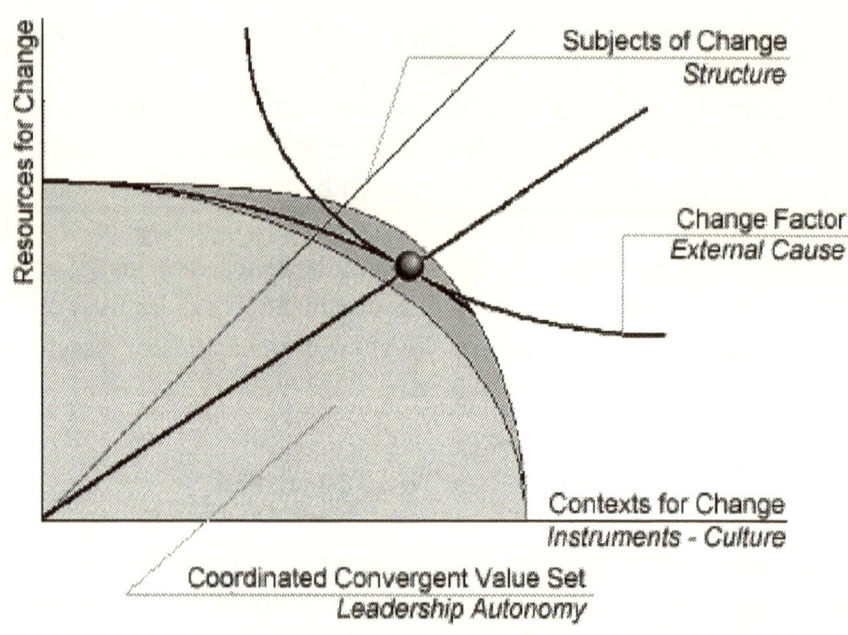

Figure 19. Leadership Challenge in Change Management

In managing fundamental change, adaptive capability is the product of a learning organization empowered by its corporate culture and facilitated by effective leadership, and leadership itself requires a learning strategy. Common but hazardous wisdom on leadership is that leadership is a matter of charisma and vision. The fact is that leadership skills are not innate. They can be acquired and built around one's charisma and vision. A leader's charisma and vision must be expressed in the values, attitudes and behaviors of those around the leader, and that means the totality of converged employee values and so forth must be represented by the leader's autonomy.

Learning Strategy in Change Management

Change management requires both leadership roles and managerial skills in deciding what needs to be done, encouraging involvement of people to accomplish the goals, and ensuring that the works actually get done. Complementary and balanced roles include, setting directions versus planning and budgeting, aligning participants versus organizing and staffing employees, and inspiring and motivating versus controlling and measuring performance.

By leadership a company first learns the nature of a fundamental change and how to cope with it. By management a company can cope with the complexity of a change that turns to new order and predictability to a situation. Collaborative roles of leadership and management can be utilized to balance the economic modeling and organizational modeling of fundamental change in businesses. By balancing the acts of leadership and management, organizations can adapt to both systemic, structural changes and organizational, cultural changes. As a learning organization, re-institutionalized standards represented by a balanced leadership and management can produce a flexible and tolerant structure and an adaptive and resilient culture in the complex and changing business environment.

III

Logic and Logistics of Metaethical Business Practices

Introduction to Logic and Logistics of Metaethical Business Practices
If You Have a Problem with Your Spirituality, Fix It before Reading

Now that the readers (herein, *you*) expect the philosophical inquiries into ethics and morality of business are about to end, the author of this book gets religious on you and starts another chapter with more spiritual terms. If you are receptive or too sensitive to someone else's religion, please keep distance from this book for a while and retrace your own paths to spirituality. Please remember, however, to return to the book when you get this idea: It is *impossible* for any of you to define morality with your human reason alone.

The meaning of morality is definitive with the ideas of deity and piety; without humility before those concepts of divinity, ethics remains as mere customs of human traditions. It is the author's intention to introduce a concept of morality with your confirmation of your own ideas of divinity, regardless of your religion or non-religion.

Notions of the fifth discipline in social sciences presuppose the ideas of what is holistic, spiritual, supernatural and divine existence of external causes. Whether or not you start your business on *calling*, you need to be aware of such external causes as long as there is someone who believes in the existence of such causes, whether that someone is your partner, client, supplier or auditor. The author assumes that, if the sole purpose of a business were to make money for yourself, you would not have opened this book in the first place. Your expectation of something *other* than making money, or the belief of something that should justify your moneymaking practices, would be the enough motive to read and think about what is being discussed in this book.

With those provisions in this introduction, the author may feel free to practice anyone's religion or spirituality in this part to discuss the logic and logistics of metaethical business practices. The discussions of business ethics hereinafter extend to the subjects of a society around a business, the environment, nature, and the metaphysics of human conscience. The author needs to take what is invisible or apparently is a matter of perception into consideration to make arguments, without which it would be very difficult to make moral justification of anyone's business practices acceptable to anybody else.

The idea of social responsibility of a business is not complete unless the norms accepted and incorporated in the business is concrete. It is overwhelming for you as a businessperson to take social responsibilities, simply because someone else may do or say otherwise whenever you do or say whatever on such subjects. However, that should not stop you to think enough is enough, because that will hold you back from expanding your moral autonomy. Even if you simply desire to become a big shot, you still need to shut them up when other people express some thoughts against you. The best way that helps you shut them up is to keep trying to be more autonomous in your own way, and the more justifiable means of being autonomous is ethical, rather than legal, fiscal or physical, because that makes you blameless, and that makes whatever you do fair and acceptable to others. You can realize how big you are when somebody else bases his or her moral justification on what you believe and reason, and that fact is available to you if you keep questioning the subjects to appear in the following chapters of this book.

15. Sound Logic of a New Business
Be Good or Sound Good

The first question to ask about a good nature of business is its *soundness*. Business well being commands this: beware and be nice to others. Not all of apparently successful new ventures, however, may embrace such a point of view at the very start. Anybody successful in his or her business affair is also capable of either expressing or hiding its reason that made his or her choice viable. To add values to your business, you need to make your logic not only valid but also sound—that is a common rule of business philosophy. Sound business affairs begin with a pledge to just pay and honest reward, so that a company's price-earnings ratio is reasonable at any rate.

A successful scheme that *sounds* good to the many must be necessitated by its aesthetic values. Buyers and suppliers of a business need to be convinced that a deal does sound good to them. Like it or not, perceptions make the soundness of a business realistic to others.

Whether being good or sounding good or both, there need to be some prescriptions at a planning phase, with or without the factual information about customers' needs and wants. In either way we really don't know which of any two ways will succeed, yet business owners must make sure that either way is operational. Here, with the use of metaethical ideas of *being* good, comes a set of standards applicable to anyone's promotional scheme: *traits*, *constituents*, and *consequences*.

Traits: Idiosyncrasy of Good Business

Even if we know by heart that we are gifted, we may have tried to reason why and how we are qualified or entitled to that something. The undergoing relationship between grace and one's integrity must be noticed before you rationalize your good traits. If you can reason yourself at higher standards, you could be more likely to be your own boss. It would not be the case, however, if your down-to-earth virtue were only worldly. In order to position yourself fair and upright between your virtue and your personal values, analyze how you can be so sure about your quality by using an ethical point of view. Then you must see the timing of departure. That ability of finding a departure point is gifted to someone who can be a good master, and if you are the one, you already know that is your talent.

Analysis of Entrepreneurial Traits

Motivating factors cited and recited by successful entrepreneurs have some common values that are significantly high on the scales of reasons for success. However, those values are still subject to any criticism and sometimes lose its meaning. Out of your good intention you may find what kind of strings are attached to your own business propositions.

Universal Being

Reflective mind on your trait can tell you about two things. You can either bet on your intuition that you are skilled in valuing art of something, or trust your understanding that you know your own virtues. Any quality that sounds merely subjective must be excluded from the checklist of your traits for now. Unless you are the Almighty you cannot form a universal norm of anything, but you can have a belief that you can try and grab its vision by aspiring yourself. Having that in mind is a good starting point to be creative.

Creative Thinking

By being creative, you can land a nice job; by creating a concept, you could be a philosopher. Creating a new concept can be a daydreamer's job, but you as a businessperson may have an urgent need to shape it into a salable object right now. Before talking about the variables and tactics used for it, first you need an abstraction. Philosophizing your own life, their lives, and experiences in business, structures and procedures of institutional causes and forces, you will start surfacing with a bright concept in hand. Creative thinking begins with either a metaphysical inquiry into something or a critical thinking of the particular, but in either way you must not project your own cause by assumptions. You might need to hypothesize a situation by constructing premises first, and you do need to prove a fact or two before idealizing your own conclusion as something fit to a market.

Problem-Solving

Anybody can solve a question in two ways: manipulation by learning, or revolution by making a difference. In either way, two things in one relation must be clear: cause and effect. Problem solving is not discounting a virtue by intuition. To avoid this fraudulent hunch you need to balance between rhetoric and foundation. You cannot solve a question only by rhetoric; nor can by dogmatic reason alone, by which you risk your flexibility and adaptability. Problem solving must function in a way that you look at the bottom of your to-do list for today and find what can be done in a routine, so that you can use the same solution to a recurring problem. You cannot always trust your instinct when you need to fix a bug in a computer program, because intuition does not help you finish a project but start a job. A problem solving skill takes more than someone's educated guess, and that needs to be proven as a fact in order to be listed as one of your traits.

Losing Control

A skill in losing control *over* something is highly recommended. Entrepreneur should not have control over everything in his or her life. Expect and anticipate the timings you have to start losing control over something you are currently tied up to. Even though you may enjoy counting the number of things and folks under your control, number is not the one you chase after. Your objective in your business is to fulfill your ideas, and you do not need to do everything by yourself to make that happen. Build a system to make things controllable with or without your presence. If you lose part of your business by losing control over something to others, you would just need to figure out which way you go next: let it go, or fire everybody else. The latter way will put you back on a starting point. A business never grows in size and shape if the entrepreneur keeps firing everybody else and no employees wish to stay with the entrepreneurs, and many businesses are just like that.

However, losing control *in* something is, on the other hand, not a good sign. If you cannot stop eating cookies till finished, you would have a problem with your health. You must have developed clear understanding of the mechanism and phenomenology of delusion. Once you notice that you are losing your control *over* yourself *in* doing something, you must start finding a way out and regaining your control. Losing yourself in a heady daydream helps create a concept, but it does not cure the damage caused by not acting on your outstanding bills. Never confuse preemptive values with opportunity costs.

Gaining control by losing it may sound metaphorical to you, but it's also real. Give those with expertise some sort of authority and responsibility they can manage in your business. Come to terms with your opponents by providing alternatives so that they are not going to have you over a barrel. Furthermore, give your experts burden of performance and keep them from interference so that they have full responsibility without an excuse. Your objective is to be on top of things but you do not have to take their jobs away as long as you stay on top of them.

Losing What You Save

Acquiring assets and resources sounds exciting, but it cannot last. Anybody who tries to save his or her life will lose it somehow. Your objective is to be adequate when acquiring something, which is different from saving it. Make sure that you have nothing to lose but to acquire when you face and present yourself to your angels. You need to make a decision whether to take somebody's wealth into nothing, or to take only your sandals and leave.

One's reasonable judgment must be sound in a reciprocal way. Whether you use the measurement of old or you have set a new standard for your business, that will be the measurement used for your practices to be justified. Any categorical imperative has its own limits set by the margin of imagination of whoever discovered it. Your standard is unreasonable unless you are ready for losing and disappointing consequences in any unpredictable circumstances. Therefore, be ready to lose it as you start adding things. This attitude makes things easier when you ponder your exit strategies.

Decision to Invest in Good Businesses

When looking for a new investment opportunity, it is wise to consider the degree of freedom found in a business or a deal. The higher the degree of freedom, the narrower the confidence interval. That means investors can be sure that a business will pay off at certain confidence level. To attract more resources to your business, you need to increase the number of variables that you can appeal to the markets, prospects, and investors. Those key variables are about your integrity—especially your *commitment*, *credibility*, and *contribution*.

Commitment

Healthy mind is raised in faith and mortal body is what you lay down in order to raise others, but your calculative mind is usually in-between and your body won't move an inch unless you reason otherwise. We are vulnerable to our own mind that lets ourselves face our own business half-heartedly. Commitment is not a value judgment but must come out of the fact that you or your idea is worth something. Commitment is that you make unconditionally even without someone else's guarantee that the fact you found is true.

Credibility

Maintain low profile as long as your line of credit is lower than how much you can handle. Do not make any false claim that you can pay any price, because no debts get unnoticed—metaethically speaking. What you have now is all you need, and your current status or eligibility is the totality of your financial autonomy, although it does not immediately set the boundary of your moral autonomy. Your constituents are those who decide how financially credible you are, and some of them might be watching your fall—and your financial domain falls into your moral autonomy by definition. This is not your opportunity to lower your moral standards unless someone guaranteed that your personal values are perceived higher than you can imagine.

Contribution

Entrepreneurs contribute their initiative, skills, ingenuity and leadership without being designated by someone else. The abundance of your contribution must appeal to others in the same field where you look for support. Your contribution is not only for your own interests but also for the ends of others in your society and neighborhood, close or distant. Without such contributions, you are someone who makes money for yourself but not for the common good. Go further to find the constituents of your business.

Constituents: Perceptions of Good Business

Find the field of gold where you get a lot of information and useful tips about how to design and package your products and services. Be ready to give control to others by listening to the people around you and by expecting criticism. You cannot come up with a concrete form of idea without any help from others, and you need to share a belief of yours because someone has already had it before with some kinds of rituals and formalities. It is to define what you have in mind is right and acceptable, by comparing yours to others.

Insight of Field of Gold &Contact of a Purifier

Your objective is to discover the discreteness of your own ideas. With a testimony of someone in particular field, whom you can trust on particular subject, you can have your concepts filtered, sifted through, and purified. Trust your hunch, but instinct is always liable to errors until you see everything.

Field of Gold

No matter how ready you are, jump out of your place and explore the field you dream of. Whether you go there by yourself or with someone else, try to locate forums and consortiums which are already networking masters and clients in your field. Finding out at what level of standards they are operating their businesses would help you get a quick insight of how far you can go, and also save your time and energy. Notice an urge to join them when you see how your competitors are doing, and start building your package as you continue surfing the network of people, till you build your commitment.

Any community or society has its norms, as well as customs and ethics. Be ready to encounter different practices that may look or sound strange and foreign to you. Analyze the validity and soundness of those unfamiliar protocols, to find out how just, fair, decent, complete and correct they are, first based on your understanding of your own ethics. With some discussion groups on particular concerns you may share useful information to help your analyses.

<u>Contact of Purifier</u>

You might already have a mentor or mentors in your field of study, but if not, pick one of your competitors or an organizer of the consortium you join. Learn what they believe and think, and how they talk, behave and do their business. Some of the prominent, experienced or skilled people may inspire you in some way, or disturb you otherwise. This experience will refuel your cycle and re-cycle of investigation. You need a view of external causes, as long as you try out your own standards by inquiring. Do not waste your time tinkering on your already well-designed piece of jewel; what detail you need to see to launch a successful venture is more likely to be found with the viewpoints of many.

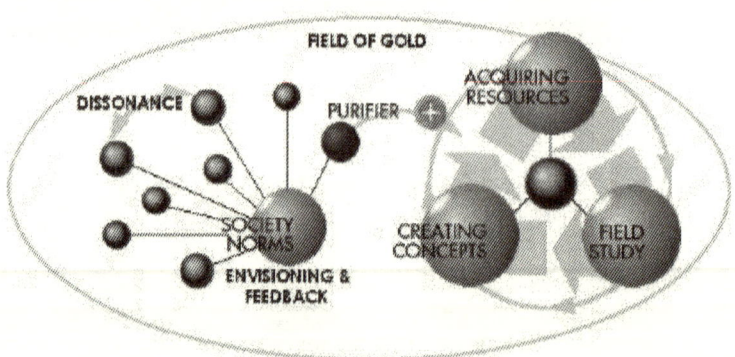

Figure 20. Roles of Constituents at Startup Phase of Businesses

Consequences: Promises of Good Business

A defect is within, but success or failure comes from the outside of your business—your constituency, based on how successful it is for your customers to project their own values or base their judgment on what you promise. In order to transcend contingency to a sure thing at your confidence level, increase your autonomous scale to absorb values and decisions of others. Whether it is a thorough life-cycle analysis or a sample polling, increase your literacy and awareness of your surroundings. Once in a lifetime, you may find yourself free from a rule of consequences, but first you need to increase your awareness to have your version of holistic view of things developed.

Perceived Sustainability in the Environment

Sustainability of your business to its environment is a sign of a sound business. It helps you confirm and nurture your commitment, gain credits from your constituents and contribute to your environment with moral consequences.

Corruption and decadence of a system, whether it's natural, social or economic, have human causes. Conflicts of different values among individuals, groups, organizations, and communities produce inequities with biased views and discriminatory behaviors. Those conflicts affect the balance in and between economic and ecological wealth that may have strong impacts on the daily life of beings as a hazardous consequence. Be sensitive enough to how others react to your propositions. Analyze such differences and variations of values, purposes and facts of life among others and find the root causes of the conceivable problems that might arise.

Increased literacy and awareness will help you find working systems and mechanisms of improving the quality of your life concerns. Conservation and restoration projects in your community and environment might be on their way to produce positive outcomes. Innovation of technology may open a new path to find solutions, and may heighten your standards of values and conducts.

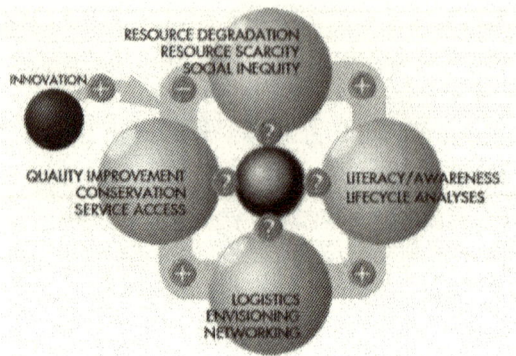

Figure 21. Perceived Sustainability in Economy and Society

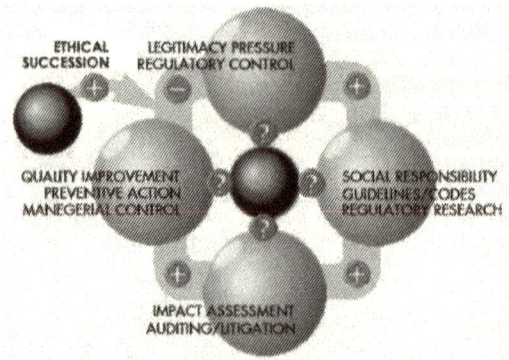

Figure 22. Perceived Sustainability in Regulatory Compliance

Roles of a Sound Business

Place any business at the center of this circle of sustainable development of its community and the environment. Think how one can participate and contribute at each step of the cycle. Before you decide to go into a circle of sustainability ombud members, however, emphasize on what are required to the participants. Here are the examples of what to be considered when you open up a sound business for the sake of sustainable environment.

Location, Location, Location

Even if you are not in a retail business, a sound business in a sustainable environment is opted for building, nurturing and curing your community values and wealth. Whether it is your PO Box address or an address in the cyberspace, be aware of where you are, what types of constituents you are going to interact, and where and whom you are going to leave behind. Choosing a location is to minimize the chances of leaving unwanted consequences in someone else's backyard.

Perishability, Intangibility, Heterogeneity

Consider how much of variety and diversity your concepts and ideas can cover and represent, and realize the size and scale of your business domain—how autonomous it is to represent such constituents from all different backgrounds. Unless your own value sets cover and represent those of others, you would not be able to come up with the ideas that produce a business that is fit for the diversity of the market. If you go one step further to form the ideas and concerns of unity, the process of planning your business will be more complicated than you can imagine.

- Perishability: make sure how long your claim or promise will last. Your logic may not remain valid when something unexpected comes up, and at that point, your logic loses its soundness. Beware of both recurrent issues and non-recurrent events to keep your logic in good shape.
- Intangibility: services often give immaterial benefit to your customers and environment, good and bad. Consequences of your business practices may or may not be visible and tangible to others, even to yourself.
- Heterogeneity: sensitivity matters to the fact that different people may take things differently. Consider whether your same products and services appeal in the same way, or you have to design and package them in several ways.

Beware of false claim

Avoid gyps of any kinds, whether they are from you, your suppliers or partners. Define, however, the difference between telling a lie and not telling the whole story, and classify every piece of information in your story in accordance with your responsibilities to others and the needs of others to whom you make a claim. State the obvious and stick to the facts as long as there is a justifiable reason for you not to disclose all of what you have. Such justification, of course, requires your ethics to be presentable to others.

Perform Full-Cost Analysis

Cash-flow analysis, break-even analysis, cash-based accounting— evaluation of ideas may take several formulas. Many business startups look at only a short-term range with a narrow scope of constituents. Conducting an impact assessment of your business will help build a better plan for its soundness. A full-cost analysis helps you look at the causes and effects in multi-dimensional ways. This includes not only regulatory compliance, but also the conformity of your business to many definitions of legitimacy—legal, financial, social, moral—that requires innovation to your own reasoning in how much of a full-cost analysis is ever enough to conduct your business.

Transcending Normative Causes with Soundness

The goal of a sound business may not only to produce wealth for its company, but for the entire community that has certain function to use and reuse its good.

One of the assets a sound business can build and use for the sake of its community and environment would be to heighten the ethical standards of its neighbors. Many people might think legal compliance as the foremost legitimacy that governs the ethics of today. In a sustainable development cycle people tend to see the consequence as the first cause, and try to maintain their actions at the level of responding mainly to resolve illegitimacy. Decreasing and resolving a crisis is a good start to solve a problem, but the ultimate goal is not to relieve illegitimacy but to uphold legitimacy; it needs to be 'not to harm' rather than harming as little as possible. As a successful and sound proprietor, you can be the purifier to one of those vicious circles of perceived sustainability.

16. Moral Causes in Environmental Disputes

Sound Moral Argument in Environmental Cases

A sound proposition for or against waste disposal and recycling is a blend of the economic and environmental arguments. First, the use of economic mechanisms is crucial for determining the value of waste management and recycling. Second, a holistic view of environmental issues must be devised in order to validate the logical scheme used in an argument. How to combine these two arguments may be within the arguer's discretion, depending on which of these two ends is to be emphasized. The argument can be either one: deducting from a holistic environmental view some economic and legislative proposals, or using particular instances, for example, the disposal or recycling of computer material, as the inference to a more metaphysical view of the environment.

Moral principles can be used either as the first principle to be reduced to the ideals of business practices, or as the main objective of a discussion to be inferred, beginning with a particular case. In either way, however, the moral principles to be used may be tainted with vague conceptualization of causes in an environmental dispute. Beginning with what is moral, what is good, reaching a conclusion about what actions need to be taken to control waste management practices can be a very long way. Whether it is a seriously planned moral quest or just as a hook in a research paper, moral principles and the methods of moral justification to be introduced need to be simple and clear.

One may suggest a straightforward way to look at the issue of waste management in a simple principle such as 'reduce, reuse and recycle.' However, moral justification of a company's practices engaged in waste management is not just about the calculation of opportunity cost and preventive remedy. Arguers need to look into the logic and applications of certain *moral* principle, such as 'not to harm others,' in many different ways.

There is a danger, both physical and logical, in making one's own judgment on how much damage is harmful. Without a simple moral cause and its clear value statement, an argument for sustainable environment can be wasted by either exaggeration of facts or subjective use of interests. Otherwise, an argument on financial and environmental disputes can be a mere opinionated debate, such as the one over soil degradation to decide if an increase in corporate taxes is a viable option to cause more environmental awareness in the industry. All the participants in the debate must uphold the principle of 'not to harm others,' instead of asking to harm as little as possible or not to harm themselves, in order to find at least a common ground of the rules to follow.

There is also a danger, both physical and logical, in making judgment on whether cloning is ethical. Without a simple moral cause such as 'to help save someone's life is ethical,' an argument for or against the outcomes of cloning would be reduced to a debate over the means: cloning as a science is the means, use of which as a purpose should matter more. A discussion of skin transplant procedures must not be misused as a debate over human cloning, even if both concern the same science, as long as the purpose of its use is to 'save' life instead of 'create' another one.

Another kind of danger, both physical and logical, is in deciding a fate of someone's life. Without a clear moral principle such as 'to have someone's life treated with devoted care,' ending someone's life is a mere legal debate. Whether such a life has the right, or categorically is a property of other, is a legal or historical issue that changes its content by region and time. Whether the act in concern is assisting a suicide or euthanasia of a pet, moral issues must be separated from legal issues, suggesting that even with the moral support from others, one must be ready for the legal consequences of one's act. The legal concern is about a 'killing' in this case, while people's moral support stems from the principle of 'devoted care.' There should be a whole set of different arguments as to define what an act of killing is and what killing is both just and legal.

Legal justification cannot supersede moral justification, while moral justification has no jurisdiction over the legal systems of a society. A clear distinction between them must be made in order to position moral concerns as primordial to legal issues, and hence moral issues need to be resolved before the legal concerns. There would be no complaint filed at the court as long as those who were affected by the act regard one's act as moral.

Some may not be bothered to do the right things without any warning signs, taking advantage of not seeing vital signs by ignoring them. Others may just try to gain control over others by increasing red tapes. Without the statements of some empirical facts, we may not care to force ourselves to be ethical, or even environmentally friendly. Otherwise, we might ask, why we should consider the interests of others in a distant place more seriously than our own. The problem is not a conflict of interests, but the lack of principles that are clear enough to be used in any meaningful discussions.

Normative measures to moral issues are distinct from legal solutions or financial remedies, and such measures have the quality to be ascribed to what is common. Moral principles are the ones to be deduced to another set of principles, but not the one to be reduced from a higher set of rules. We do not expect to reduce billions to one in order to come up with certain moral rules, but to unify the many to define a common order. Likewise, we do not expect to eliminate others, neighbors, species, races, or habitats in order to establish our ethics, but to integrate different customs into one simple moral principle in order to make a case that would affect inconceivably many others.

17. The Art of Communicating Ethical Values in Public
Ethical Business Propositions at Work

Balance between the Subjects of Ethical Business

Suppose your business plan is up—both in your conscience and in your package of words, graphics, and actions. When you are determined to identify yourself and your business, however, make sure that your business contains unceasing message to the world, in simple and clear terms. No categorical concepts formed by philosophers are flawless. Nor any categorized promises made by businesspeople can last forever or be kept up-to-date to the changing values of their customers.

To make sure that your propositions are fit for the market, a message that your business conveys needs to be constantly checked its communication value. It also needs to be revised and properly rephrased, and if necessary, be removed. In order to make your moral communiqué contemporary, you must maintain the validity and soundness of your proposition all the time, while you base your judgment on the moral principles that do not change over time.

A critical issue here is who cares to listen to your message while your prospects are not necessarily concerned about your moral principles. Your potential customers need to know what kind of tangible benefit you can offer with your products and services. Once you start selling ethics in the first place, you almost start to fail in reality. First of all, ethics or wisdom is not what you sell, but is the knowledge to buy, build and acquire. Also, not many ethical ventures for profit are destined to succeed, because their ideas are often hard to be formed into tangible substance. In your scheme of persuasion you may assume that some-body might desperately listen to you, or that your voice must be heard because you speak of truth. Hold that thought and save your breath, and do not jump to assumptions until you make the fact of your serv-ices and make sure your audience know that fact.

First you need to slow down your passion and emotion, but instead show to others the promise of results. You still have to expect misunder-standing, misinterpretation, indifference, or even disgust or objection, but that should not lead you to a scheme of deceit and bait. Strategy should not hold your standards down.

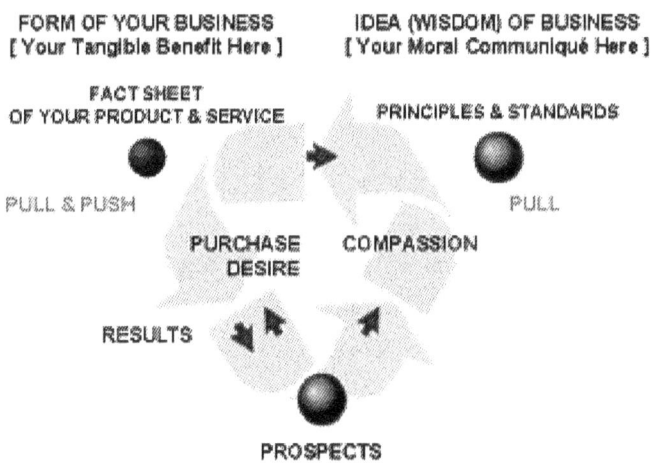

Figure 23. Balance between the Subjects of Your Talk
(Benefits of Your Business and Philosophy Behind Them)

The truth you need to hold lies not in manipulating your ethical standards, but in balancing your conversation between the subjects and contexts, because behind the facts of your business or services stands the philosophy and principle of your own. Facts can be pushed in an envelope, or pulled as a string, but your principles and ethical standards can only be used as a string to pull, otherwise your message will sound dogmatic and turn off the audience. Let them buy your ideas by having them ask you to present, because your ideas are the soul of business, not for sale but the instrument to invite someone else's compassion.

Conversations that revolve around your own personal plans are often likely to spark off intriguing ideas, when you are insightful and quite familiar with the subjects you are discussing. By luck you might make a very good first impression that may drive your long-term vision working in your favor. However, in communications morality is not what you show off in words but something to be observed by someone else as you act on it. You do not sell your ethics, but sell your character, because you can only negotiate by representing the power of virtue but by the power of position where the virtue itself rest. Your powerful character is a tool to display your understanding of ethics and wisdom; you are not the wisdom yourself.

Art of Communicating Your Ethical Values

A great challenge to businesspeople is being capable of identifying what they offer. Effectively articulating the uniqueness and necessity of your business offering requires that your communication be memorable, believable, and credible.

Making Impressions [Memorability]

Let us take the advice that the first impression is a lasting one. How can we, then, make that first impression memorable?

Even though a perception can be reality to many people, words that sound fresh do not necessarily sound realistic. Words written in contemporary language and spoken by the prospects can be sound and healthy, and may be memorable, but you may worry that your copy sounds like a cliché.

The importance of a good first impression is often misunderstood because the notion is built on a weak logic of a premise that uniqueness leads to memorability, or that remembrance follows notability. Unique messages convey two different qualities: a memorable quality by being anecdotal, so that it serves in experience of its audience, and a memorable quality by reflecting the sender's unusual characters so that the audience can expect something new. Uniqueness of the sender's character can be invisible at a glance and can be implied comparatively by using customary characters that the audience can experience.

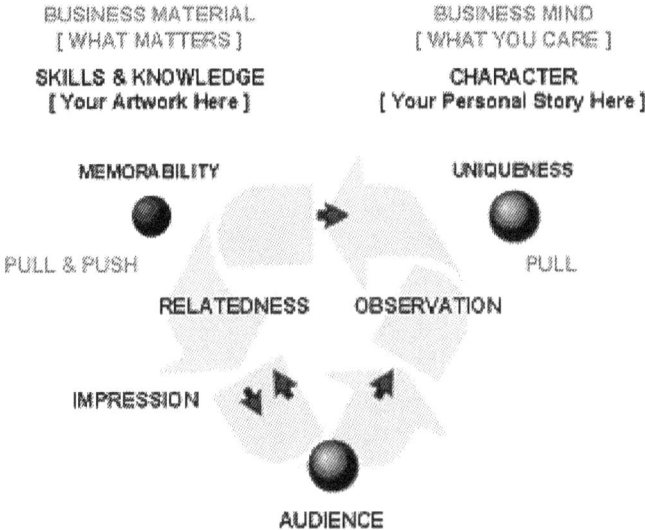

Figure 24. Art of Communicating Ethical Values: Memorability

Stating Contents Decree [Believability]

Now that many of those unique phrasing tactics became just a bunch of cliché, it may not be easy to talk about the contents of your written or verbal communication of your products and ideas. As in writing a résumé, many would recommend to throw out generic use and meaning of words and to turn into powerful and relational phrasing when writing a positioning statement. It is necessary that your product or service be differentiated by strong propositions and be referred to your prospect's personal experience. But do powerful words and phrases such as *finally*, *at last*, *now you can*, and *absolutely*, really sound unique to you?

A specific use of general and definitive terms does not necessarily associate with your prospect's sensory experience, because the logic built for such an association is weak and unsound. Justification of the use of such words and phrases must be based on the fact that the association between the meaning and the experience hold. If all your analyses come short of one explanation that your product or service has certain *absolute* value or advantage, your meaning of the word loses its soundness. It does not matter anymore even if you spent a long time on your segmentation analysis of the served and un-served markets, your knowledge of psychological mechanism of human needs and wants, or your understanding of cultural and value differences among people.

In metaethics, it needs to be a fact but not an assumption that a use of language is a matter of choice and its context is a matter of expression made for particular target audience. Moral justification must be based on a fact, and your justification of using certain word to certain audience must be proven effective. However, you may not assume that would work on different subjects in different contexts. Each case must have a proof of fact, so that you can justify your promise to anybody in any contexts in your market. If that seems impossible to reach at your planning or starting phase of your business, then refrain the use of definitive words, in order to make your proposition valid and sound, so that your promise is believable.

Sensitivity only is not enough, because you are responsible for many consequences of writing a short positioning statement of your business. Check back your statement and try to prove its assertions to be metaphysically correct and metaethically sound. Then do the same to your business propositions so that in time you realize your conviction is true and unique.

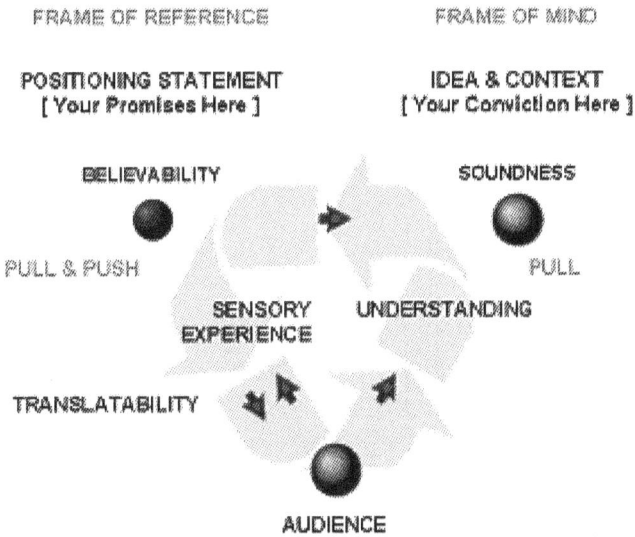

Figure 25. Contents of Business Communication: Believability

Communicating Your Business Mission in Public [Credibility]

Writing a mission statement in 25 words or less may sound easy, but by doing so you may have to reduce your character, if you are producing a short statement by reducing the words from a longer statement. You may not reduce your principle to find a short cut, but you need to expand your statement by applying your principle to practices.

Maximized expectations among prospects will amount to your credibility. A clear mission statement is an indication of your philosophy and reason that give your audience a hope that their faith and belief will be assured with your confidence. A mission statement is not an expression of your own passion, regardless of how strong it might be, but the statement of your contributions to your audience based on your knowledge and experience that can turn their faith or belief, regardless of how vague that might be, into an assured thought, which corresponds your own conviction. Such a statement of contributions makes you appear credible to your audience, because with your valid knowledge and experience you can make your conviction sound.

You do not want to reject your prospects with your arrogance or intellectual pride that may create vanity. You need to state your mission in terms of your contributions to others, not as your bogus proclamation of your belief, because the audience may look for every chance to question that you are a false prophet.

While being rational can be fallible and deviant from accuracy when relying on too easy frame of mind, as shown in the above analyses, being idealistic can be far from facing reality. One most important thing to avoid when communicating your ideas can be to make unrealistic expectations among prospects, given that your statement proves to be believable. The sound logic of being a good salesperson is to state with validity how good is what you offer. Credibility can be gained without taking things personal by unnecessarily revealing who and what he or she is.

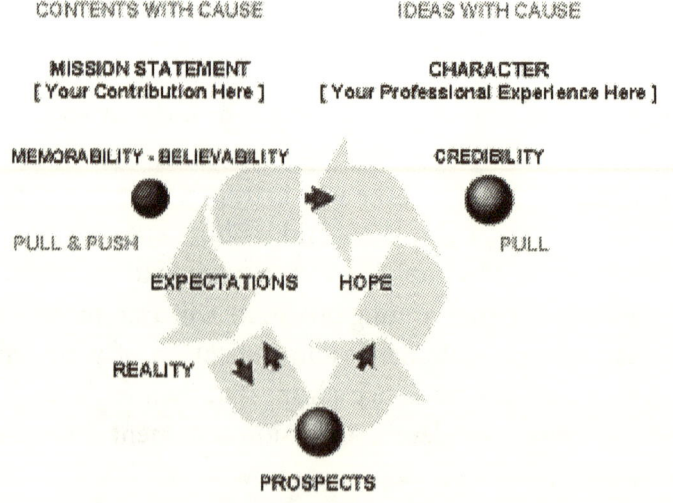

Figure 26. Communicating Your Mission: Credibility

18. Pseudo Symmetries of Human Factors
Symmetry in Ergonomic Perspective

The final chapter of this book is dedicated to an experiment of how far a business can go to make its propositions metaethically valid and sound. In this chapter, the author argues that the soundness of a business is found in a concept of symmetry, among other dreams and promises of balance and equilibrium, and conducts a case study of the existing products to demonstrate how fair they could be. The whole study may sound nonsense, and the author has no intention to break the rules or the harmony and comfort we already have in our material life. This chapter is intended to challenge the human factors that instantly accept *de facto* standards as customs, because the concept of such customs do not guarantee the ideas of fairness. Please try to have fun.

If you ever tried using *right-handed* scissors with your left hand to cut a sheet of paper, you might have noticed how difficult it is. Since many tools and machines are designed for right-handed users, many left-handers have been left with few choices besides learning how to use tools with their right hand. Ergonomics may often be considered the knowledge and applications for human factor engineering. But such *factors* that we presumed effective and efficient for most of the time did not necessarily address the interests of all kinds of people, right and left, tall and short, young and old. It is hard to find universally ergonomic products in the market; some people might even say there are no such things.

As a central idea concerning the abilities and limitations of humans, ergonomics has had its cause from the times of our ancestors, but it has only recently become a body of knowledge with conceptual foundations. Nowadays ergonomic design is an established field of study for applying knowledge to designing tools and systems, physical and mental, natural and social. Using machines, systems, and environments of our time have become much safer, efficient and effective, and more comfortable to many of us.

Ergonomic product designs still need to include more human factors left out for a long time—those of structural minorities, or of anatomical irregularities. It is not necessarily about the design for the handicapped and the disabled; some users are simply left-handed and otherwise can keep up with the standards. What is introduced here a concept of *symmetry*, the geometrical regularity of form. Since the system of our human body and mind is roughly symmetrical, differentiating right from left may not give much weight in human thoughts. However, building integral views of human bodies and their functioning in ergonomics requires much more metaethical inquiries.

Ergonomics in Asymmetries

Symmetric form is a form left unchanged by motion, either by reflection, translation, or rotation. Reflection or translation, which is to interchange energy and substance between equidistant points on opposite sides, is an operation that results in unchanging the form it takes. Circular motion on a circle or a sphere also preserves the beauty of its form by rotation. In designing an ergonomic product, however, we need to consider how much of such purity our human forms and systems can acquire in reality. Human bodies have a dialectic system of differentiating right from left: human brain has two hemispheres; human consciousness has a struggle between body and mind; what one's heart prompts versus what his or her mind tells, and so on. We have a trouble with telling our left hand what our right hand is doing. Human factors of such right and left imbalance suggest broken symmetry or imperfect symmetry of our systems, physical or socio-economic. Hence it is quite difficult to devise such things as perfectly symmetrical and perfectly ergonomic designs of a system. It is a fact that any ergonomic design has its own contexts and conditions, and therefore an answer to building an ergonomic product requires some kind of arbitration.

However, applying the functions of symmetry is ideal when a concept of unity is preferred over the facts of diversity. Perception such as ease of use is often subjective, but if a product is designed for the particular, ease of use can be a false frame of reference because its meaning and merit stay at the same point. Design may start from having in mind a particular use, but ergonomic designs are the instruments of integrating such particulars, small or large.

Here are some examples of how we misunderstand or simply missuse the concept of ergonomics.

Example 1. Ergonomics in Asymmetries

Most products for either home or commercial use are designed for right-handed users, even if they are considered ergonomic—designed to reduce possible physical or mental harm. For example:

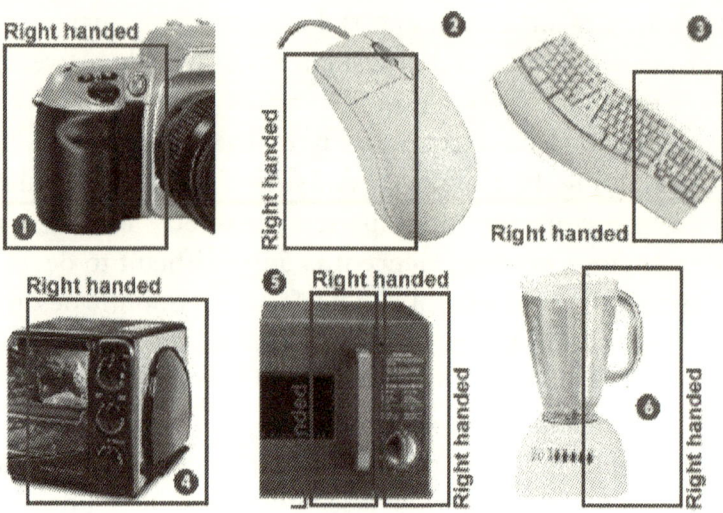

Figure 27. Ergonomics in Asymmetries

1. A shutter release button of a point-and-shoot camera is located at the top right hand side of the body. If a user feels more sensitive when using left hand, this product design may compromise artistry of the photographer.
2. Computer mice, although the buttons can be switched for left-handers by setup, may not always come in symmetric shape. Since many users share a device in public, left-handers may not always have a choice.
3. A computer keyboard, such as the above, may or may not have a symmetric layout. Needless to say, ten keys are usually located at the right hand side.
4. Home-use oven toasters are compact, and in many cases buttons and dials are located at the right hand side of the machine.
5. An oven for commercial use, if it does not have switches and handles on top, such as the above, may cause certain problems to left-handed cooks, at least in terms of convenience as well as space efficiency.
6. Handle at the right side of a jar, such as the above, may not concern most users who are right-handed. It could be placed the other way,

but what do you feel if you cannot see the manufacturer's logo or instructions that are printed on the *front* side?

Example 2. Ergonomics in Asymmetries—2

Check out the web page on the screen you are now looking at—is it designed for right-handed or left-handed folks, or both? Look how frames are designed, as well as the browser screen itself. If you are using a mouse with your right hand, you may not sense any uneasiness. If you are left-handed, or if you do contrary thinking in your brain, however:

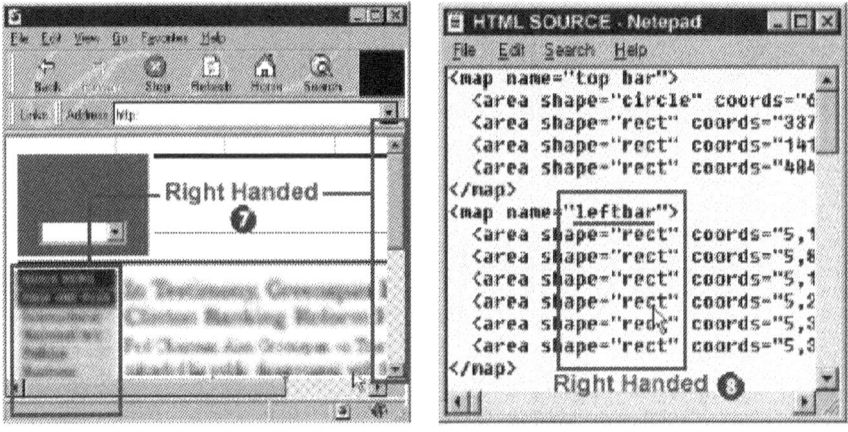

Figure 28. Ergonomics in Asymmetries–2

7. Scroll bar of a browser must be at right, so that a right-handed mouse user can easily touch the bar. Likewise, a navigator frame on the right hand side? No, that must be on the left hand side, because articles at right could be much longer than navigator bars or a map, vertically, and the reader's attention should be on the article than the menu bar. Scroll bars could be placed on both sides of the screen, but who dares if it reduces the display area?

8. An HTML source for a web page (unrelated to No. 7). The navigation map is called 'leftbar.' For anyone who is accustomed to certain

left-to-right or *top-down* ways of listing things, it may sound rather just *natural*—how about if *your* common language is Hebrew or Arabic? Would you consider switching from right hand to left to redo everything?

Example 3. Ergonomics in Symmetries in a Collective Sense

Scissors at your home or in your office might be right-handed, but there are *left-handed* scissors available, thanks to the craftsmanship of manufacturers. Such tools and devices as scissors can be designed exclusively for left-handed users. Here are some examples:

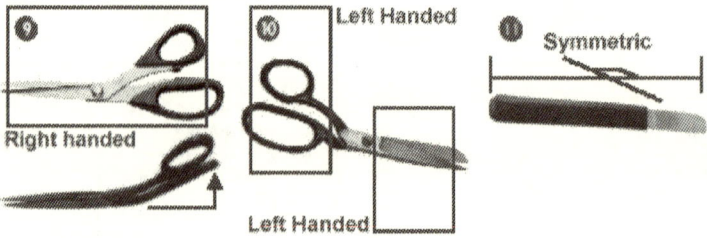

Figure 29. Ergonomics in Symmetries in a Collective Sense

9. Right-handed scissors, as usual.
10. Left-handed scissors. You could use right-handed scissors with your left hand, but you might have to cut a paper in *bottom up* way, which may be difficult and could cause pain. Since the scissors above are designed for left-handed users, they can be considered highly ergonomic for the left-handers.
11. A knife can be used either with right or left hand, and you might not feel left out if you find a manufacturer's logo on both sides of the knife. Unfortunately, this is not always the case.

Example 4. Ergonomics in Symmetries

How blessed are the athletes. Beautiful symmetries such as the following are possible in sports arena, thanks to the strict rules of the game.

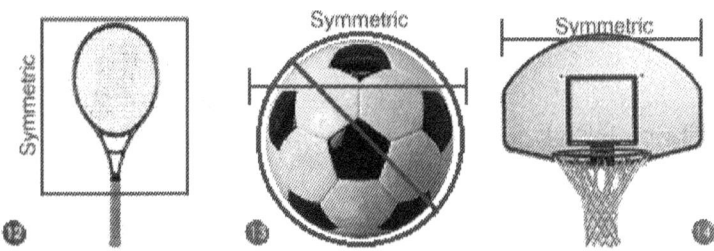

Figure 30. Ergonomics in Symmetries

12. A tennis racquet. The same racquet can be used either with right or left hand—the only difference is, which side is smooth or rough.
13. Obviously, a sphere provides perfect symmetry, either in rotation, reflection, or translation. A soccer ball is a good example.
14. In a basket ball game, players can shoot either from right or left. A backboard is designed as above by rule.

Human factors, physical and social, or large and small, have innate disparities of right and left. Even apparently ergonomic design may have lots of drawbacks to left-handed users, and that is because, unfortunately, our first hand experience of tools blurs clear understanding of symmetry. That is to say, our experience interrupts a process of defining what is. First hand experience amends the first principle of what is to the level of what makes sense to the particular, by instantly discounting a higher value and then projecting a product of one's own value judgment.

Ergonomics in Quasi-symmetries: Trick of A Circle

As long as our cognitive abilities are close enough to reality, we say a circle is the ultimate form of symmetry. This does not guarantee that any forms in circular shape can keep the promise of ergonomic symmetry. A soccer ball may do, but not a clock. A ball does not rotate in particular direction but any. A clock does, by design, rotate in particular direction, because our perception of time has a value that increases without being reversed. By definition it is not symmetric if something changes its form by rotation. Change in geometric value brings increase or decrease in the sum of angular momentum when a clock goes or a runner in a baseball field moves, and this means that symmetry has to be broken in order to give nature change in its value, positive or negative.

Example 5. Ergonomics in Semi-symmetries

It is true that a circle is perfectly symmetrical and uniform. In the cases of a clock, a baseball field, and a dial switch on a machine, however, things are not uniform. They go either clockwise or counter clockwise, and that has already broken the symmetry a circle is supposed to provide.

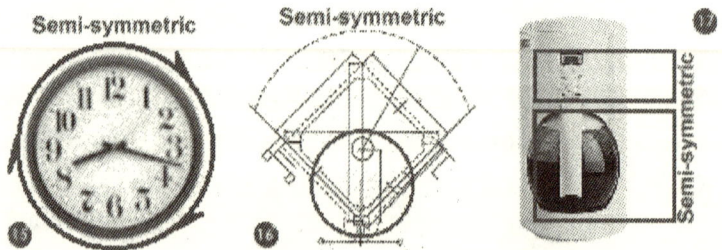

Figure 31. Ergonomics in Semi-Symmetries

15. A wall clock. Here we are not just to look at the shape, but the value that increases as time goes by. The shape of this wall clock is symmetrical, since it's a circle, but giving it a clockwise move, we might

notice what's asymmetrical in a circle. Imagine a volume dial on your analog stereo system. If you are required to turn up the volume, which hand would you use? If your left hand has to turn clockwise, isn't it much harder than turning it down? Please try it.

16. A diagram of baseball field. It looks circular and hence symmetrical, but the runners are, according to the rules, supposed to run counter clockwise. This is because an ordinary man or woman can turn left much easier than turning right.

17. A coffee machine with a switch and a pitcher handle located at the center of the machine's body. See how the dial switch works—clockwise or otherwise? If you are using your left hand, you might have to strain your wrist and elbow by twisting it a little too much.

Ergonomics in Perspective: Concept of Metaethical Symmetry

Once a state of symmetry is assured, a clock stops, or any motion on a clock gives no difference in time. In symmetry time does not matter as much as it does in our conceivable universe. All individuals as many as number n in a universe with $(n+1)$ dimensions share the same value with or without meeting a half way, and time loses its significance. Any motion along a circle gives no difference in value as long as symmetry is preserved. Such a state is possible only if supersymmetry is in effect.

Imagine a pigeon in apparently symmetrical shape steps on a volume dial of a stereo system and click it. When it uses its right foot to click a dial its body moves down to its right, that seems to us natural. When it uses its left foot to click it, its right side of the body gives inertia and the pigeon has to twist its left foot a little harder. If we knew only certain distance along the circumference of a circular dial is mostly in use, we could design it as the volume zero is located at such a point that reduces stress on user's left hand. We do not need to locate the minimum volume and the maximum volume of a dial in symmetrical way, which simply tricks us by confusing pseudo symmetry of right and left positions with ideal state of circular equilibrium.

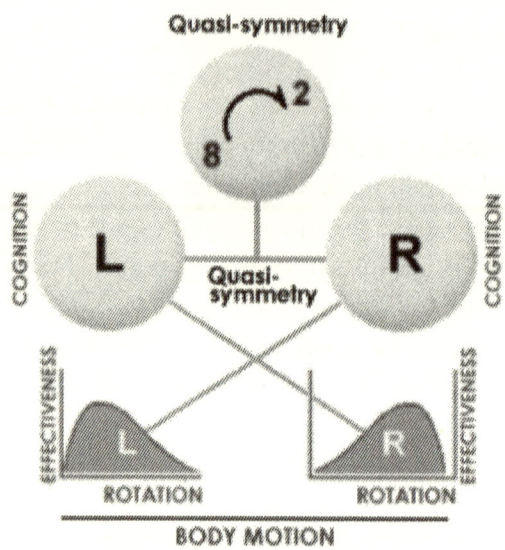

Figure 32. Quasi-Symmetry and Effectiveness of Rotation

Our body has only rough or semi symmetry between right and left, and performance or effectiveness of right and left are not always synchronized. When the right only steadily increases its efficiency or momentum during a rotation on a circle from eight to two, clockwise, the effectiveness of the left is at its highest point as it moves the same way. To give a device ergonomic use value, is to devise symmetry of right and left at its most attainable level of effectiveness for both at the same time. It requires fair understanding of circular symmetry and emptying prejudice of our right hand experience.

There is no perfect symmetry in human factors, but our increased awareness in the ideas and functions of symmetry gives a great starting point of ergonomic design. We would notice a significant advancement in ergonomics once we see a clock dial on a device that is as much ergonomic as a tennis racquet. Truly ergonomic design needs to get out of the field of athletes, where the social conditions are reduced to uphold the rules of the game. A sound business affairs begins at the principle and extends its reach by expanding the area of applicable rules, and so the ergonomic design be considered principal over a game strategy.

Afterword
Abstraction of Sound Business Practices

Judging between legitimacy and illegitimacy could, unless it's done thoroughly enough, rather creates an inertia that holds back a business and a corporation from uplifting the company's values to higher standards of norms. Compliance to the regulations of our society may switch our focus from ends to means—although we might be busy enacting quality control, we may end up mistakenly clearing all the important issues across the border of assembly lines.

Deductions and reductions are the norms of logical thinking, and the moral principles can also be reduced to something other than moral. The logic of sound business practices, however, begins with defining moral principles as given concepts, and neither deductions from other concepts nor projections of subjective values can be used to confer or infer the concepts of morality as the secondary reason.

Validity and soundness of a moral justification in a business can be suggested only by integrating the structures and conditions of our social systems with the intrinsic values of the available resources, the operation that generates the model and perception of moral autonomy, which sets the ethical standards of a given system. Such standards are only the approximation and representation of the moral principles, and our standards of living by social conditions do not override the concept of what is moral. With that humility before the ideals, our judgment must follow the form, and our mission is to dare to care and try harder, without compromising by falling under the structures and the conditions of legitimacy pressure.

Free exercises of metaethical inquiry in the field of business and social sciences do not necessarily put the companies out of business. The choice in a business is either/or if the soundness of the business is concerned over its validity, and those who dare not to care about the causes to serve the greater common good may simply miss the opportunities of making progress of different kinds, conceivable only by constructing the fifth dimension of the universe. Social sciences face their own limits when someone tries to proclaim morality and ethical values within the scope of social sciences. It can be, however, a philosopher's job to counter offer as a nonphilosophy to comprehend the philosophy of social sciences.

The author differentiated morally irrelevant businesses from ethically sound businesses. For the readers of this book, the choice is clear: stay where you are and you can still make money. The idea of sound business practices may seem a rotten idea in social sciences. Such characterization is valid, but possible because of the framework of social sciences. The author may call it a value judgment, and simply point out its danger, because it could cost you if a value judgment does not sound good to you. It would cost the author if the idea does not sound good to you—but I thank you for finishing this book at any cost.

The Author,
December 2002

0-595-26469-7